Mobile Marketing In A Week

Nick Smith

The Teach Yourself series has been trusted around the world for over 75 years. This new series of 'In a Week' business books is designed to help people at all levels and around the world to further their careers. Learn in a week, what the experts learn in a lifetime.

Nick Smith runs Traxxon.co.uk, a digital marketing consultancy specializing in helping UK companies increase their sales and profits using a combination of search engine optimization, social media marketing and media buying.

Nick is also the author of other books in the series including: *Social Media Marketing In A Week, SEO and Search Marketing In A Week, Digital Marketing In A Week* and *eCommerce In A Week*.

Mobile
Marketing
In A Week

Nick Smith

First published in Great Britain in 2019 by John Murray Learning. An Hachette UK company.

British Library Cataloguing in Publication Data: a catalogue record for this title is available from the British Library.

Library of Congress Catalog Card Number: on file.

ISBN 978 1 473 60750 7

eISBN 978 1 473 67731 9

1

Typeset by Cenveo Publisher Services.

Printed and bound in Great Britain by CPI Group (UK) Ltd., Croydon, CR0 4YY.

John Murray Learning policy is to use papers that are natural, renewable and recyclable products and made from wood grown in sustainable forests. The logging and manufacturing processes are expected to conform to the environmental regulations of the country of origin.

Carmelite House
50 Victoria Embankment
London EC4Y 0DZ
www.hodder.co.uk

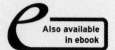

Contents

Introduction

The other day I was walking through my local shopping centre and I saw a mobile virtual reality headset for sale – the type that you put your mobile phone in and instantly get transported to another world.

I grew up in the generation where things like that were the stuff of the Jetsons or Thunderbirds (now that's aged me). I grew up with *Encyclopedia Britannica*, the *A to Z* and MS-DOS.

I know what it means to have to go to a library for research, and how to properly cite something (but don't ask me to do it now). I know what it is like to have dial-up internet.

Heck I can remember connecting to bulletin board systems via a 1200/75 modem just like in the *War Games* movie! Ask any kid on the street today and they will have no idea what you're talking about.

Now I have all the world's knowledge, whether from Wikipedia, from the online *Encyclopedia Britannica* or some other source, constantly updated every second of every day ... in my pocket.

With my phone I can video chat with friends and family anywhere in the world and I can pop it into a headset and have virtual reality within seconds.

I can ask my phone to not only tell me how far away a specific location is, but also give me directions to it.

The phone I have right now blows away the laptop I used five years ago and could probably run 99.9 per cent of my daily business tasks (short of using Photoshop) on it.

Things are moving scarily fast. Like 'blink and miss it' fast. Especially when it comes to mobile. Right now more than two-thirds of all internet traffic in the USA is mobile (http://bit.ly/2NhKL1T).

On Black Friday in 2018, $2 billion in online sales (a third of all online sales in that 24-hour period) came from smartphones and other mobile devices, a 4.5% increase from 2017.

The following Cyber Monday was even bigger generating online revenues of $7.9 billion, with 54.3% of all visitors coming from mobile devices. Source: http://bit.ly/2R8wNFJ.

These trends are becoming a wave, and we businesspeople better learn to surf it or we'll be crushed by companies that do. The world isn't going to stop because of my age or experience and it won't stop for yours.

If you're reading this book you are most likely in the same boat most business owners are in: trying to figure out what the heck is going on, and then trying to figure out how to generate revenue with it.

While I am far from a 'guru' or 'master' in this domain (as if anyone can be since these trends started happening practically yesterday), I *can* help you apply solid online marketing principles to this new 'mobile' generation.

The key is not only knowing how things are changing, but more importantly how people's minds are changing with them, because marketing is mostly a psychological game.

When you know that, you'll be in a better position than your competitors.

Blessed are the flexible for they will not be broken.

So prepare to enter a whole new world.

Let me know how you get on: nick@traxxon.co.uk

SUNDAY

What's the big deal with mobile?

It is inevitable.

Two reasons:

1 Technology: Mobile internet speeds are getting faster and data compression is constantly improving.
2 Cost: It's never been cheaper to get online. You can buy a decent, no-contract Android smartphone for under $100 (at the time of writing).

I could also go into detail about the law of accelerating returns and direct you to an excellent but dryer-than-the-Sahara technical article, but the main reason it will happen is because people *want* it to.

The fact of the matter is, there are BILLIONS of people around the world who are happy to spend countless hours scrolling through their newsfeeds and watching cute kitten videos on their smartphone every day.

I'm not ashamed to say I love my smartphone. I was with a friend the other day listening to some music streaming in from a radio station *on my phone* and he wondered out loud who had just sung that song. I fired up my web browser *on my phone*, did a quick search for part of a lyric I managed to remember and within a few seconds I had the answer.

The future is mobile

I use my phone to connect with my project manager and staff when I am on the road. I can even work on my laptop at my desk at home while riding in a car using TeamViewer or LogMeIn apps.

If I wanted to I could probably write, edit and format this whole book on my mobile phone using Google Docs Voice Typing function. It doesn't require any training to recognize my voice, is very accurate (minimal corrections) and is completely free! No matter where I am in the world, I can dictate a chapter into my phone, make any edits I want, and share the document in the cloud with my editor so he can see in real time what I am doing. (Err, not sure I should have mentioned that as it might give him ideas.) Do that and 'BAM!, I have a chapter in maybe an hour or two of talk time, and then I can put my feet up, call it a day and relax.

Here's a list of some other (not all) ways the world is going mobile and will continue to do so over the next few years:

Knowledge is mobile

People may not know where a business or organization is located or what the capital of Venezuela is, but they do know *where* to go to find that information. Instead of having to know everything, they can whip out their mobile phone and hit Google for the most current information.

Do you remember the last time you looked at an encyclopedia? Nope, me neither. They don't even make the physical Britannica encyclopedias anymore. They went the way of the dodo thanks to Wikipedia.

Photographs and images are mobile

Instagram, Facebook, Flickr and more all cater to a market that uploads photos on the go. Almost every smartphone now has a camera in it that can take photos almost as well as a dedicated digital camera. In fact, digital cameras themselves are becoming more of a professional product than a consumer product, as shipments of all digital cameras have dramatically fallen over the past eight years from a peak of 121.5 million sales to just 25 million in 2017 (source: https://read.bi/2Neg1iw).

Video is mobile

The sheer size of statistics covering online video is mind-boggling.

- More than a BILLION hours of videos are watched on YouTube every <u>day</u>.
- According to Cisco, by 2021 a million minutes of video content will cross global IP networks every <u>second</u>.
- Over half a BILLION people are watching videos on Facebook every <u>day</u>.
- 72 hours of video are being uploaded to YouTube every <u>60 seconds</u>.

Not so very long ago, if you wanted to film something, you used your camcorder. Not anymore. The latest generation of smartphones can shoot in 4K (four times higher definition than Blu-ray discs) and if you need an even more professional result, you can purchase all manner of semi-pro add-ons like high-quality lenses, stabilizers and drones to get those sweet aerial shots.

So-called 'action cameras' like GoPros let you attach your tiny video camera to your bike or your helmet strap and record your activities. And with a click or a tap, you can upload the finished results to Facebook, Instagram, YouTube etc. and share your creations with the world.

If you don't want to mess about with editing your footage, you can always livestream to millions of people from your phone or GoPro and becoming your own TV channel.

If that's not your bag and you just want to stick to watching TV and movies, no problem. Most TV companies have sections on their website or dedicated apps that will let you catch up with your favourite show you missed a couple of nights ago, which you can watch on your phone. There are plenty of dedicated movie apps like Netflix, Amazon Prime Video and Sky Cinema, where you can get your movie fix (not to mention exclusive award-winning and highly-regarded TV shows they produce themselves), all available on the go through your smartphone.

Books are mobile

During 2017 (the most up-to-date figures at the time of writing) 55% of online book purchases were e-books (source: authorearnings.com). You may have seen stories in the news talking about the 'death of e-books' and the resurgence of print. This isn't telling the whole story.

It's true that e-book sales from major publishers *have* been declining mainly due to them increasing their prices but when you include e-books that are self-published, independently published or published directly by Amazon total US e-book sales *rose* by 4% (source: https://ab.co/2P59Z5n).

As nice as it is to snuggle up with a book, people find it just too much to cart around hardcover books. It is much easier to buy it online and download it on whatever e-book reading device they own.

Navigation is mobile

Just as stand-alone, digital cameras are dying, so are stand-alone GPS sat-nav systems like TomTom and Garmin. Thanks to most smartphones today having built-in maps and sat-nav systems and a plethora of third-party apps and services, all designed to help you get around with minimal disruption, sales of dedicated sat-nav fell from a peak of 48 million units in 2011 to just 3.2 million units in 2015 (the most current figures available; source: http://bit.ly/2xU8mRK).

Notebooks/cabinet files are mobile

Not only are the obvious things going mobile, but even note-taking via Evernote, Dropbox, Microsoft's OneNote and other services are making documents and notes you have made accessible with just a few taps of your finger.

Wonder if that invoice has been paid? Check your Dropbox...

Did you write something down on a piece of paper but are worried about losing it? Break out your smartphone, snap a picture of it and have it instantly uploaded to your Evernote account, which will automatically use writing recognition software so you can search for the note later by typing in a few keywords.

Magazines/newspapers are mobile

Print is dying a slow and painful death as pretty much every publication is going digital, and by extension also going online and mobile. No more inky fingers or having to queue to get your morning paper while you wait for your train.

Why wait till tomorrow morning to find out what is happening in the news today, when you can find out instantly on Twitter from news organizations or the papers who print it?

You can get up-to-the-minute info simply by grabbing your phone, heading over to BBC News, CNN or Reddit.com to find out all the info the papers won't have for another 24 hours.

All via mobile technology.

Thinking like the mobile generation

I have gone to great lengths here to show that everything which can go mobile is going mobile. So what does this mean for your business? It means you *need* to start thinking about going mobile as soon as possible if your market is heading that way. Position yourself early or you will find yourself playing catch up, and I'm talking about much more than just having a mobile-enabled website (which of course you should have).

Studies have shown that our brains literally change shape and pathways depending on the technology we use (source: http://bit.ly/2R2bUMs) and in time this will also change our psychology.

Most people do not buy rationally but through their emotions, then justify their purchase with logic, and as such you need to make sure your mobile visitors *feel* right when they visit you.

Let's look at this in more detail:

The mobile customer wants things fast

Everywhere and in every way speed is becoming more of an issue. In many places around the world, truly unlimited 4G mobile data is becoming a reality.

Your customer is now carrying around something that can (to all intents and purposes) tell them anything they want to know, and they are now learning that it can get them anything they want – fast.

Customers want instant gratification and their smartphone allows them to get it! Same-day delivery is already available from some companies on items as large as refrigerators if you order before a certain time, and Amazon is experimenting with same-day delivery using a fleet of drones to carry packages, so they can get purchases to their customers as quickly as possible.

If ecommerce companies are looking into using drones to transport items, you can bet your bottom dollar couriers like FedEx, UPS and DHL and even postal companies like the UK Royal Mail will also be looking into it to stay competitive.

As bonkers as thousands of unmanned drones criss-crossing the sky sounds, these companies are continually looking to the future and you should do the same.

I'm not suggesting you must invest in a fleet of drones but you need to take it *very seriously* that your customer wants things as fast as is physically possible. If you're not able to deliver fast and your competitor is, you're in for a painful time.

The mobile customer wants a simple user experience

When you start attracting mobile traffic to your business, you need to make sure the process for the customer to complete the order or gather more information is as ridiculously easy as possible.

It's better for both parties if the user creates an account for your website so they can repeat order quickly and so you can follow up with additional related offers. But if the customer has to create an account to purchase that teddy bear for little Angelina, and has to type on their smartphone while they're rushing to catch the next train home from work, it is going to be a nightmare for them if they have to manually enter all their information by hand and are suffering from constant FFEs (Fat Finger Errors). As one of the twenty-first century's greatest thinkers once said, 'Ain't nobody got time for that!'

Your customer *will likely* give up and find someone else selling that teddy bear who's a darn sight easier to order from. You need to remove as many reasons for them to type whenever possible.

For instance, instead of forcing users to manually enter their data, give them the option to create an account using their Facebook, Twitter, Google or Instagram accounts. Or if you're using an ecommerce platform like Shopify or Magento you can use plugins and extensions to automatically copy over customer information into a mailing list provider like Mailchimp for you to send follow-up offers.

And don't stop with account creation and the ordering process. Make sure your customer support options are also dead simple. Put your contact phone number front and centre on your website in the mobile browser. Make it so they can call with one touch.

Give them options to email you, text you, Facebook message you, Tweet you etc. Think about the networks and services your customers use every day and make sure you're there and contactable.

Just being quickly reachable is such a ridiculously simple step towards giving amazing customer service that I'm surprised it's still not the norm. It doesn't have to be super technical or convoluted. A simple statement on your website like:

'Any problems? Text, Instagram, FB Message or email us your order number and the problem and we'll get back to you ASAP!'

And lastly, make sure you have a much-simplified version of your website showing when someone visits on a mobile device with everything laid out as clearly as possible.

Make it fast to load and cut out anything that doesn't absolutely need to be there: 53% of visitors to a mobile website abandon it if it takes longer than three seconds to load. For every second delay it takes to load the website, conversions fall by 12% (Google, 2018).

If you don't have a ton of money to invest in a mobile version of your website with all the ordering functionality, just have people call you to place their order.

(IMPORTANT: Speak with your credit card processor first to make sure you're allowed to manually enter your customer's credit card information.)

Ideally this shouldn't be the only purchase option you offer as not everyone will be comfortable giving their credit card information over the phone, but it *is* a quick and simple way for some people to order without you having to spend a ton of money having something coded.

Think of it this way: if someone has never been to your mobile website before, will they be able to figure out where they need to go in as few clicks or taps as possible? Ask friends and family for *honest* feedback on your mobile website. Once you've ironed out all the issues then you may have a winner on your hands, so make it live and see what happens. Ask your customers what they think – offer them a discount for any help they can give.

Any time you offer a discount to someone for their help, if your discount system is computerized, make sure the voucher/discount code can only be used once per customer. That way they can't take advantage of you or share it around the internet. If it's not computerized, just keep a simple Excel spreadsheet of all the people you've given a discount to and how much and check all orders against it. When they've ordered, delete them from the spreadsheet.

The mobile customer wants it the way they want it

Not only do your customers want something fast, they want it fast and ideally *customized* to them. If you sell ties and people want a 24-inch, green and yellow polka-dot, waterproof tie, you better make sure a) the ordering process is super-easy and b) you give them customizing options (HINT: people pay more for custom stuff).

Technology has made it possible for users to customize their day-to-day mobile experience. They can see the posts that they want from friends/pages that they want. A few taps and they can see the latest weather reports for their area, which movies starring their favourite actor are on at their local cinema or on TV tonight and so on.

This means you need to offer flexibility. Where can they change their order? Can they have it in a different colour? Different size? Do they want it gift-wrapped? With a personalized note? What can you offer to make a purchase more special for the customer before their order goes out the door?

This is where it is good to keep up to date with not only what's possible in your industry but also in other industries.

An example

You have a dog grooming business. What could you do to save your customer's time? Could you offer a mobile version of your service?

1 Just the fact of coming to a customer's home means less time spent and inconvenience of having to catch little Fluffy and get them to you and less stress for Fluffy being in an unfamiliar environment.
2 The VIP same-day service: Great Aunt Mabel just phoned and has invited herself round for dinner but Fluffy looks like she's been out chasing rabbits around the woods. How are you going to cook dinner *and* clean Fluffy? No problem – if you select the VIP option and contact us before 12pm, we'll come to you today.

3 Give customers a simple process to sign up for an account, give their phone number and address, set the time when they want you to show up and what style they want Fluffy coiffured into. There are always a million options here but pick the most common options that most of your customers choose (think of the 80/20 rule).

I know the above might be a bit much to do all at once but the key is to focus on one step at a time and you will already be light-years ahead of your competition.

OK let's go start attracting these mobile customers!

Summary

The aim of this chapter has been to point out how the advances in mobile technology are rapidly changing the way we interact with each other, our purchasing behaviour and the effects (positive and negative) it can have on our productivity.

We often take technology for granted and don't notice its effects on our day-to-day lives, but to maximize our business successes, it's vital we try to see where it is ultimately going and, most importantly, profit from it by positioning ourselves and our businesses correctly.

A massive shift is happening and when it is complete it will seem like it happened 'overnight' while you were sleeping.

Don't let this happen.

Using the examples in this chapter, start thinking about the various ways in which you can reach mobile users today. Pose this question to your subconscious as you drift off to dreaming about puppies and rainbows ...

'How can I make my business(es), better positioned for the mobile future, starting tomorrow?'

Keep this question in mind while you go through the rest of the chapters, tweaking and adding to it as you progress.

Fact-check (answers at the back)

1. How many hours of video are watched on YouTube every day?
   a) 10 million ❑
   b) 1 billion ❑
   c) 270,000 ❑
   d) 14.67 ❑
   e) 100 million ❑

2. In 2017, e-books made up what percentage of online book sales?
   a) 46% ❑
   b) 27% ❑
   c) 55% ❑
   d) 9% ❑
   e) 34% ❑

3. Most people do not make rational purchasing decisions. Instead they purchase using:
   a) a credit card and hide the bill when it comes in ❑
   b) logic and then justify with emotion ❑
   c) with cash ❑
   d) emotion and then justify with logic ❑
   e) instinct ❑

4. What was the *Encyclopedia Britannica* killer?
   a) WhatsApp ❑
   b) Facebook ❑
   c) Wikipedia ❑
   d) Twitter ❑
   e) MayoClinic ❑

5. Which options should you give customers to contact you:
   a) Email ❑
   b) Phone ❑
   c) Twitter ❑
   d) SMS/Text ❑
   e) All of the above (and more) ❑

6. Mobile users want their products:
   a) Slowly ❑
   b) Fast ❑
   c) Instantly ❑
   d) b and c (if possible) ❑

7. Mobile users love complicated and hard-to-navigate websites.
   a) True ❑
   b) False ❑

8. Do mobile users like to give things a custom spin?
   a) Yes ❑
   b) No ❑

9. What is one way to get feedback on your website?
   a) Ask family ❑
   b) Look through the site and guess ❑
   c) Ask customers ❑
   d) a and c ❑

10. One question you can ask yourself to appeal to the mobile consumer is:
    a) How can I make things more complicated? ❑
    b) How can I make them more money? ❑
    c) What can I do to save them time? ❑

MONDAY

Simple mobile SEO tactics

It doesn't matter how great your website may look or how fast it loads, if nobody knows about it – it might as well not exist.

One of the most effective tools to bring a continual stream of prospective customers to your business' website is from a specific search that's performed in one of the main search engines like Google, Bing or Yahoo.

However, as search engines have billions of results in their indexes, today's business owner must use a mix of art and science to attempt to reverse-engineer the secretive algorithms and ranking criteria Google and others use to determine which of your webpages is seen by the search engines as the most relevant result for a query.

This reverse-engineering strategy is called search engine optimization, or SEO, and today I'll cover some of the simple things you can do to increase your chances of generating visitors for little or no monetary cost by using mobile-specific search engine optimization (SEO).

But first here's something you probably don't know ...

Mobile traffic

If you have a website, you're almost certainly getting mobile traffic in some form already.

Don't believe me?

Go into your analytics software (which is probably Google Analytics since it is the most popular) and look at your visitors. Now look at the types of visitor to see whether they're mobile devices or not...

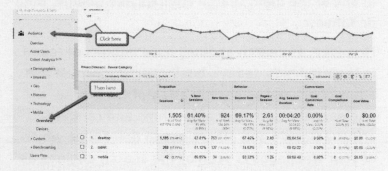

You probably have a good percentage of mobile visitors. When I randomly check the stats for my websites, I can see around 15 per cent of my traffic is mobile.

The truth about the mobile internet is that *it is the internet now*. This shouldn't come as any surprise. Mobile internet usage overtook desktop internet activity back in 2016 (source: http://bit.ly/2Cu98sk) and the number of worldwide smartphone users is forecast to increase from 2.1 billion in 2016 to 2.5 billion by the end of 2019 (source: http://bit.ly/2IIGbcC).

Sure, many of those users have both but the reality for a lot of people is it's more convenient to surf the web on their tablet or phone. And now the mobile market has matured, people are more confident with purchasing goods and services using their phone, especially with the development of Wallet apps built-in to iOS and Android, and technologies like Near Field Communication (NFC) enabling people to pay by physically touching their phones to a keypad to send payments.

Now that mobile users are becoming a higher quality visitor, you're not limited to which type of traffic you get: whether it's from Google search results, social media or from paid media (Google AdWords, Facebook Ads, etc.).

Before we look at how to use Google to get your business in front of your audience on their mobiles, it's worth spending a little time defining exactly *who* your audience is.

I'm not talking about people aged between X and Y, or 'Millennials', I'm talking about fleshing out your audience by creating a customer avatar – an individual persona that describes your ideal customer in detail.

Why go to all this trouble? Once you know exactly who your buyers are, their behaviours, where they go online, what their hopes and desires are for using your product or service etc. then it becomes a lot easier for you to market to that 'person' – make sense?

Creating your customer avatar

To create your customer avatar, start by thinking about the primary product or service you're offering. If you have existing customers go through their information and pull out any data you can think of that might be useful. If you can find them on Facebook, look at their occupations, the kind of things they like. Are there any common denominators?

If you don't have any customers yet, guess as best as you can. If you're still drawing a blank, hire someone from a freelancing site like UpWork.com to help you create an avatar.

Now write a short biography about your ideal customer. Use the following example to help.

Hoboken Dog-Grooming: customer avatar

Customer data reveals that, for a dog-grooming business based in Hoboken, New Jersey, most customers are women aged between 35 and 44 who live within a 20-mile radius.

This is just an example: yours will probably be less detailed than this in the beginning but you can build it up as you add to it over time and as you learn more about your audience.

When crafting your avatar, be as detailed as possible with the data you have or can find – try asking questions such as:

- Would Jill and Mike be interested in this?
- Will it save them time or money?
- Will it be entertaining to them enough that they take a minute to watch a quick video?
- Would the headline catch their attention if they happened to see it while browsing YouTube?
- What about the video thumbnail image?

If it doesn't appeal to your customer avatar, then you need to go back to the drawing board. You need content that is laser targeted to your avatar, not boring, generic messages.

Leveraging mobile search

With more and more people surfing and searching from mobile devices, it's important to do everything you can to take advantage of these users. One of the best ways is to optimize the pages on your website to show up in the Top 10 results when people enter a specific search term. This is known as search engine optimization (SEO).

There are certain things you need to make sure you've done in order to optimize your webpages for organic search (i.e. the main results section, not the paid ads at the top or bottom) and there are additional things you need to do to optimize for mobile search.

TIP *We will look briefly here at how to optimize for mobile search, but for more in-depth information (and when it comes to SEO, the devil really is in the detail) I highly recommend grabbing a copy of my companion title* SEO and Search Marketing In A Week.

Title and description meta tags

Title Tag
The Title Tag is the text that displays when you hover over a tab in your browser and is one of the primary methods Google uses to try to figure out what the page is about.

Keep your Title Tag to no longer than 70 characters with important keywords towards the beginning. Every webpage on your site should have a unique Title Tag and should only focus on one main keyword at a time.

Description Tag

This is commonly used by search engines to describe what the page is about within its results.

```
<meta name="author" content="Lucy Alexander">
<meta name="description" content="Find out what digital marketing is today, the tactics involved, the types of
content you can create, and the purpose digital marketing serves to your overall marketing strategy.">
<meta name="generator" content="HubSpot">
<title>What Is Digital Marketing?</title>
```

What Is Digital Marketing? - HubSpot Blog
https://blog.hubspot.com/marketing/what-is-digital-marketing ▾
26 Jun 2018 - Find out what digital marketing is today, the tactics involved, the types
of content you can create, and the purpose digital marketing serves to ...

Digital marketing - Wikipedia
https://en.wikipedia.org/wiki/Digital_marketing ▾
Digital marketing is the marketing of products or services using digital technologies,
mainly on the Internet, but also including mobile phones, display advertising, ...
Digital marketing · Digital marketing system · Digital marketing engineer · Promotion

What is digital marketing? | SAS UK
https://www.sas.com/en_gb/insights/marketing/digital-marketing.html ▾
Learn all about what digital marketing is from our marketing insights – and find out
why it is so different from traditional marketing. Read more!

It's best practice to keep your Description to around 150–155 characters with each webpage having a unique Meta Description and a call-to-action (CTA) within it.

Also having a CTA like 'Click here ...' is incredibly important because Google tracks and compares the number of people that click each link in their results pages. If your link gets more clickthroughs than your competition, and people stay on your site, Google will reward that link with a bump in their search rankings because it's more relevant to the original search query.

Google does NOT like multiple webpages on the same site having the same Meta Title and/or Meta Description.

Hoboken Dog Grooming: Title and Meta Description

TITLE: Peggy's Pooch Pampering: **Hoboken Dog Grooming** Expert

DESCRIPTION: Peggy's is Hoboken's favorite place for coiffured canines since 1989. As used by Jersey Shore's Snooki. **Click here to get the first trim free.**

Image Alt Tags

Make sure the *alt="one-of-the-search-terms-you-are-trying-to-rank-for"* markup is added to each main image on your webpage to help give Google more information on what your webpage is about.

NOTE: Do Not Spam each image with multiple keywords or keep using the same keywords in each image. Related ones in other images are fine.

URL canonicalization

This is just a fancy way of saying 'make sure Google knows which webpage URL is the correct one'. One of the most common errors I see is unnecessary URL duplication. For example:

- http://yourdomain.com
- http://www.yourdomain.com
- http://yourdomain.com/index.html
- http://www.yourdomain.com/index.html

and so on ...

This happens a lot, and over time people or staff enter the wrong URL into local online directories, posting a promotional article on a third-party website. I know and you know they all mean the same thing (i.e. your homepage) but sometimes Google sees them as distinct, individual webpage URLs, so you need to let Google know which URL for each webpage on your website is the correct one.

Fortunately, this is easily done with one line of HTML code in your page:

←link rel="canonical" href="http://yourdomain.com/page-name"/→

Put the correct page URL in the 'href' section and paste that code above the closing ←/head→ line in your page's markup.

You also need to decide on one URL format to use across your entire website, whether it be:

- http://yourdomain.com

or

- http://www.yourdomain.com

This again confuses Google and makes it think you may have duplicate content on your website, for which they will 'penalize' you.

 I talk more about important Google penalties you need to pay attention to, like Panda and Penguin, in **Successful SEO and Search Marketing In A Week.**

Speak with your web developer about setting up your webserver to use one format or the other. For Linux-based webservers, this is done with 'htaccess' and for Windows servers it's the 'web.config' file.

Mobile friendly/first design

One effective way to generate more traffic is to make your website display nicely on mobile devices as Google is currently rewarding websites with a slight nudge in rankings if they're designed to be mobile-friendly (source: http://bit.ly/2R7tDlF).

If your website uses a popular Content Management System (CMS) like WordPress, or you have a third-party ecommerce system like Shopify or BigCommerce, you may already be generating a mobile-friendly version of your website or store. If you're not sure, ask your web designer.

If your website is not generating a mobile-friendly version, then a quick fix can be as simple as creating a 'mobilized' version of your website without any unnecessary bells and whistles and adding two small lines of HTML; one to your main webpage and one to your 'mobilized' version.

On your main/desktop version of your webpage add the following line underneath your Description Meta Tag:

←link rel="alternate" media="only screen and (max-width: 640px)"

href="**http://m.yourdomain.com/page-1**"→

Swap the **URL** for the mobile version of your page which in this case is in a subdomain on your website called "m" (your web designer can set this up).

On the mobile version of the webpage put a Canonical tag as mentioned above.

←link rel="canonical" href="http://yourdomain.com/page-1"/→

This will stop Google getting confused with two different pages having the exact same content on your website and tell them that the desktop/main version of the webpage is the page they should index.

And because Google is dang smart, it should display the mobile version of the webpage for people searching Google on their mobile.

Mobile first

If you don't currently have a website but are looking to build one soon, my advice isn't just to make it mobile friendly, but to make it 'mobile first' – in other words, build the site to be optimized for mobile as the priority – not desktop computers – right from the very beginning.

And honestly, I'd seriously consider redesigning an existing website to be 'mobile first' so you can get a massive jump on your competition by giving your ever-increasing mobile visitors a better experience.

Google's Snack Pack and citations

This isn't really talked about a lot but if you offer products or services to a specific geographic area and you aren't actively leveraging the Snack Pack then you're missing out on a lot of potential Google love.

Well, let's remedy that right now, shall we?

Google's Snack Pack/3-Pack

This appears mainly when you're searching for a type of business in a local area, so for example, the screenshot overleaf shows what comes up when I search for 'dog groomer Hoboken NJ' on my Samsung Galaxy S9.

There's an obvious ad at the top, which a lot of people just ignore but then we have a map with three businesses listed on it and directly below that is a box with more information about the businesses, like their opening times, and a convenient 'tap-to-call' button on the right.

This is the Google 3-Pack (sometimes known as the Snack Pack) and it's important to try to get into the Snack Pack for a couple of reasons, the main one being that on most modern smartphones it will appear 'above the fold' (on the screen without scrolling).

And as you can see, it's designed to be quite eye-catching so wouldn't it be better to also be in the Snack Pack so the user doesn't scroll past it to get to the regular organic search results where you're fighting with nine other results, instead of just two?

So how do you get into it?

First you need to set up an account on Google My Business (google.com/business). Go through the whole process. Fill in all your business information and request the postcard to verify your address – should take about a week to come through.

SUNDAY
MONDAY
TUESDAY
WEDNESDAY
THURSDAY
FRIDAY
SATURDAY

Look at your competition's category in the Snack Pack. That's the category you need to use too. If you're not sure, Google released a complete list of all the correct GMB categories to use for each country. See: http://bit.ly/2Rds99H

Now you need to generate local and business-related citations.

Citations

A citation is just a link from an authority website that is either from your locality, your industry or ideally both. The types of citation link you get differ according to your location and your product. For example, for the best citation sources by US city see: http://bit.ly/2R9W02o.

These are constantly changing so doing searches for terms like 'best US citation sources' or 'best UK citation sources' will help get you started. For business-related citations, think about professional bodies like associations, trade journals, respected niche directory websites etc.

As a rule, I aim to get as many highly authoritative citations as I can, with a minimum of at least 50 as the first target. Finding and submitting all the relevant citations will take time, so outsource this to a staff member or alternatively use a third-party freelancing website like UpWork.com or Fiverr.com.

Reviews

From what we know, getting lots of positive reviews doesn't seem to have a massive direct impact on your rankings within the Snack Pack. For example, I searched for 'emergency dentist Liverpool' and the results showed a website with three reviews and a 2.7 out of 5 outranking one with nine reviews averaging a 4 out of 5 (see overleaf).

However, common sense tells us that more good reviews will make our listing stand out, and make our business seem like a better option compared to our competition and hopefully generate more clicks to our website or calls to us.

The Rules

Google are just as hot on people trying to 'game' review getting as they are with other spammy SEO practices so first here's what NOT to do:

1. Compulsory: Don't incentivize people with money or anything else to write reviews for your business or write negative reviews to your competitors.

2. Compulsory: Don't hire third-party companies to create fake Google reviews. They might be under Google's radar for now, but should they be found out all companies that used them run the risk of being penalized.

Best case scenario: you lose all the reviews you paid for (wasted money).

> *Worst case scenario:* Google bans you from the Snack Pack and applies a site penalty that affects your regular rankings.
>
> Don't risk it.
>
> **3. Compulsory:** Do not set up a specialized area or kiosk in your place of business for gaining customer reviews. The main reason this isn't a good idea is that it's trivial for Google to detect this since all the reviews would come from the same IP address as your business and would be an immediate 'footprint'.
>
> **4. Advisory:** Try to avoid running periodic 'big push' campaigns to generate reviews. Having a sizable number of reviews suddenly appear on your listing looks suspicious to Google and might be mistaken for trying to 'game' the system.

So what are the best ways to get reviews? Just keep it natural. For every new customer you get, ask them if they would leave an honest review on Google.

This gives you a normal pattern of reviews, spread over time from lots of different residential IP addresses within a local area.

NOTE: If you're a business that services customers or clients over a larger area or nationally, don't worry – Google will know to expect reviews from all over the country and not just one local area.

Printed reviews

If you have customers that come to your place of business or you deal in mail order, you can give them a printed sheet that asks for the review along with instructions on how to do it.

TIP *For an online Review Handout Generator see (free account required): http://bit.ly/2R8y6ED.*

Online reviews

Once you are verified in Google My Business, you can generate a 'Leave a Review' link for your website with the following free online tool that will take the visitor directly to the review form for your business: http://bit.ly/2R8mwcy.

To make it easier to remember and to use in print, get your web designer to set up a redirect to the link using a URL like: http://yourdomain.com/review.

Dealing with spam/fake/bad reviews

Not everyone is going to like you or your business and nowadays they can instantly vocalize their displeasure by leaving a negative review in any number of places: Google, Yelp, Facebook etc. If you're actively promoting yourself or your company, as sure as 'eggs is eggs' you are at some point going to run into this issue but don't worry, it really isn't the end of the world.

Before you run screaming to Google, Yelp or whoever to attempt to have it removed think carefully if it's a legitimate complaint. If it is, reply and apologize publicly for it. Do whatever is possible to rectify the situation as best you can. Can you offer them a refund of the item or give them an additional something at no charge? If you're offering a service, can you do something else for them at no extra charge?

No business is perfect but by publicly apologizing and showing that you're trying to make amends helps when other potential customers and clients look at your reviews and see that you care about them.

If the review looks fake (i.e. doesn't talk about a specific order, is vague) then in as unbiased way as possible, check the review against Google's Review Posting Guidelines here: http://bit.ly/2Rc7qCO.

If you still feel you have a case, then click the 'Flag as Inappropriate' link next to the review explaining *specifically* why you believe it should be removed. Google will check the review and if they determine it's violated the posting guidelines, they'll remove it but it's not guaranteed.

TIP *Google won't remove bad reviews when companies and customers disagree on specific facts as they have no way to verify them.*

Summary

There has been a lot for you to take in at one time here. So let me sum it up as best I can:

First, using your analytics software, check how many people are visiting your website as a mobile user (you probably already have visitors from this whether you know it or not).

Second, create your customer avatar so everything you do from here on out is targeting the right people. You don't want to aim for everyone in the world because only a certain percentage of the population will even think of buying from you. If you are a dog-grooming service, believe it or not, not everyone owns a dog, much less a dog that needs grooming, so make sure you are targeting all your ads and website right.

Next we went through a whole bunch of technical stuff that is all important so don't skip it. Meta Tags, canonicalization and citations, etc. really do matter a lot if you want to get mobile traffic at all.

But don't get lost in it.

If you are not a technical person just give this book to your techie and let him or her

SUNDAY

MONDAY

TUESDAY

WEDNESDAY

THURSDAY

FRIDAY

SATURDAY

have it (or buy a copy for them). If you don't have a techie on hand, find someone on Upwork.com you can outsource the tech stuff to (more on this later).

We also talked about getting reviews: what not to do and what to do. Always keep in your mind 'Would Google (or whoever) think I am trying to 'game' the system?' You may be asking for an honest review but never give the customers an incentive of any monetary value and never ever use a review service.

Make it your goal to choose one suggestion in this chapter and start on it now. Don't try to get everything done in one day – do one bite-sized chunk each day.

Fact-check (answers at the back)

1. What is the most popular analytics software?
   a) Clicky ❑
   b) Piwik ❑
   c) Tableau ❑
   d) Google Analytics ❑

2. To find out who your customer truly is you need a customer:
   a) Avatar ❑
   b) Example ❑
   c) Sample ❑
   d) Survey ❑

3. You need a 'call to action' in your Meta Description because:
   a) It is cool and all the cool people are doing it. ❑
   b) It makes people more likely to click on your listing ❑
   c) Google can read it and know you are better than your competition ❑
   d) It makes your website better. ❑

4. Title and Meta Descriptions should all:
   a) Be the same on every page of your site ❑
   b) Include as many keywords as possible ❑
   c) Be unique and only target one keyword at a time. ❑
   d) Be 200 characters long and full of only your contact info. ❑

5. Images should be 'tagged' with:
   a) One keyword each if possible ❑
   b) Descriptions of the images ❑
   c) Random words ❑
   d) There should be no tags. ❑

6. You should never tell Google which webpage is canonical. You should just let them figure it out themselves.
   a) True ❑
   b) False ❑

7. Websites are all mobile-friendly automatically.
   a) True ❑
   b) False ❑

8. To get Google reviews you should:
   a) Set up your profile on Google My Business. ❑
   b) Avoid spammy ways to get reviews ❑
   c) Get reviews naturally over time by asking everyone to leave a review. ❑
   d) All of the above. ❑

9. To increase the number of reviews you get, you should:
   a) Tell new customers ❑
   b) Tell old customers ❑
   c) Hand out printouts showing people how to do it. ❑
   d) Set up sections of your website and emails to your customers with the info. ❑
   e) All of the above. ❑

10. If you get a bad review:
    a) Panic ❑
    b) Ask for it to get removed immediately ❑
    c) Flag it as spam ❑
    d) Deal with it by trying to set things right first. ❑

TUESDAY

Social media marketing

> *'It takes 20 years to build a reputation, and five minutes to ruin it. If you think about that, you'll do things differently.'*

It's seems obvious that this quote from billionaire investing legend Warren Buffet would apply to every aspect of your business (and your personal!) life – what you do and are seen to being doing have consequences and repercussions. But in the online world, these ripples are instantaneous and can reach from one side of the world to the other – in a matter of *seconds* and are archived, copied, retrieved and distributed forever.

But as powerful a tool as social media is for being able to cause huge damage to a company, when used correctly it can really pay off in a massive way and today I'm going to explain how to achieve this. Not only that but I will show you how to connect with mobile users through social media.

Benefits of social media in the mobile marketing mix

When it comes to using social media, it's important not to expect an immediate return on your investment and effort. It's not as simple as spending money on ads and then checking how many sales you have made. Social media doesn't work that way.

It is going to takes time for you to build your following, for people to get used to seeing your company name in their various feeds. It's not something that happens overnight (unless you're very lucky!).

So what are some of the benefits you can get from utilizing social media?

Building your brand

Social media is a powerful tool for brand building. It allows you to determine how you want to position your company to your target audience. It enables you to tell people about your business and highlight the people in it. Using social media effectively means you can describe and show the benefits of your products or services to your target audience. It only takes a small amount of effort and content to really make an impact.

Exposure

It's said that for a customer or client to buy from you, they had to have been exposed to your marketing messages anywhere between six and twenty times. Social media allows you to generate a *lot* of repeat exposure.

Depending on how long your average sales cycle is, it's possible to get in front of your potential customers, and clients, eyeballs tens if not dozens of times (maybe even more?) educating them on what your company can do for them.

If your products and services appeal to a wide number of different industries and you produce stellar content, who knows – it ends up being shared virally all over social media, doubling if not tripling (more?) your exposure.

Building relationships

Social media is all about building relationships, whether it's with existing customers or prospective ones. People can follow you and you them. You can find out what they like, how they use your products, how your services improved their lives or business. It's incredibly powerful. Here's a simple example:

Let's say you're perusing one of your best clients' Twitter feed on your phone and you notice they're a Chelsea supporter by the number of times they comment about the club's performance. How gobsmacked do you think they'd be if you sent them a Chelsea shirt signed by their favourite player as a birthday gift or just as a random 'Customer Appreciation' thank you? Do you think that would make them more or less inclined to do extra business with you ... or refer your company to their business colleagues?

How many other companies out there do you think are cultivating their business relationships in that way? How often has that happened to you? Yeah, me too.

Happens all the time ... Not ...

Though to be fair I did get a nice paperweight from a realtor once.

With social media you have instant, in-depth access to your followers, customers and clients who then become members of your community. Through social media, you can find out what they like, and what they don't. What they love and what drives them mad. Can you discover a gap in the market no-one is filling just from your followers' frustrated Tweets?

This level of communication and research used to take a lot of time and cost a lot of money with specialist firms but now you can accomplish almost as much with just a few social media accounts and it doesn't cost you a penny.

Establishing authority

Social media works especially well for helping companies in the business-to-business (B2B) space establish their authority on their chosen topics. Whether you're a coach, a consultant, service provider or speaker it's simple to leverage social media to 'prove' to your market that you are an expert on your subject.

All it takes is getting content out there in your area of expertise and soon enough your audience will be trained to think of you as the 'go-to-guy' or 'go-to-girl'. If people have questions, try to answer as many of them as possible – leave no question behind.

The more you can demonstrate your authority and expertise, the more content your audience will be exposed to and the easier it will be to attract new prospects, clients and other potential business partners to get in touch.

Generating website and mobile traffic

Social media when done correctly can increase the traffic to your website. However, although it is great for sharing information, sometimes it doesn't give you enough 'space' to be able to say everything you want to say to educate and inform your market. It's at times like this that you want to try and drive followers from your Facebook Page (for example) to your website.

One way of doing this, if you're a service provider, is to write (or have ghostwritten) a list-based article (for example '10 greatest myths about XYZ'), go into detail on the first three, then if people want to read the rest, have them click a link to a post on your website that goes into more detail about the other seven. You can offer them a video which goes into even more detail, or a checklist, schedule or blueprint they can print out to get a specific result, in exchange for their email address – which you can then use to keep in contact with them to offer more useful articles and just follow up with them.

Reminder: you won't get floods of traffic and new leads overnight but you don't want to either. Do you want 10,000 tyre-kickers or 500 buyers?

Competitive advantage

So many businesses still think social media is a 'fad' and that it won't amount to anything. What they don't know but I (and now you) know, is that over the past few years, social media has graduated from a digital water cooler where we hung out with our friends to talk about last night's episode of *Breaking Bad* into a serious influencing factor when it comes to buying decisions.

- Four in ten social media users have purchased an item online or in-store after sharing it or marking it as a Favourite on Twitter, Facebook or Pinterest.
- 91 per cent of global users access social media via mobile (source: http://bit.ly/2Nus6Af).
- 71 per cent of consumers are more likely to make a purchase based on social media referrals.
- 78 per cent of people say companies' social media posts impact their purchases (source: http://bit.ly/2IMeBeg).
- 81 per cent of people said recommendations and posts from family and friends on social media directly impacted on their purchasing decisions.

And don't think this behaviour is limited to consumers: if you're selling products or services to other businesses, you need to pay close attention.

- 84 per cent of C-level/vice president executives use social media to support purchase decisions (source: http://bit.ly/2OGIjXN).
- 75 percent of B2B buyers are influenced by information they found on social media (source: http://bit.ly/2ONEH6d). So it's important to offer assistance to people asking questions to prove your expertise.

I could go on but you get the point. *Social media isn't going away* and with more and more pressure on executives to do the job right the first time, social media as a research tool for B2B and B2C customers is becoming ever more important and you need to treat it as such.

Spend the time and effort to answer the questions coming in. Keep your pages and accounts updated with new content. Take social media seriously, because if you're doing a great job and your competition aren't, you'll be leaps and bounds ahead of them, giving you a great competitive advantage they'll have trouble fighting against.

Content

We've talked about how effective social media can be for pretty much any type of business, but now we need to address the elephant in the room: content.

There's no getting away from it, you are going to have to create and publish content on a regular basis to have any kind of success on social media. When I say 'you' what I really mean is:

1 You
2 Someone in your company OR
3 A person/people outside your company tasked with the role

No matter who does it, content *must* be created because without it, you're not going to show up in anyone's personal Newsfeed giving you exactly ZERO exposure.

The name of the content game is to make sure you're publishing high-quality, relevant content on a regular basis that will keep viewers interested in your business and what's going on.

How often should you publish? There's no right or wrong answer to this, but for most businesses it's better to post daily or at the very least three times a week to ensure you're not far from your target audience's thoughts.

Regardless of how often you decide to post, make sure you're consistent and do whatever you can to make sure you post on the same days every week. That way you'll be 'training' your followers to come back to your Facebook page every time some new content is due.

And always remember to remind them to come back … 'That's it for today's post. See you on Friday for this week's Friday FAQ when we'll be answering the question …'. If you *do* decide to alter the publishing schedule, give your readers plenty of notice to get ready for it.

Publishing quality content really isn't that hard. Here are a few pointers:

- Keep it relevant to your business and to your audience. Don't start posting up random funny or 'cool' videos you've seen. Your readers are coming to you for information and education on your field of expertise. If you start posting things that aren't relevant, you may lose them.
- Write in a normal, conversational manner. Don't be too formal with your language as that puts up a subconscious barrier between you and your prospect but at the same time, don't be too 'chummy' with them either. We're looking to build mutually profitable business relationships here.
- Post photos and where possible videos. People *love* to see video. Image and video content make up a large percentage of total social media content.
- Facebook's 1.57 BILLION daily mobile active users are estimated to generate around 8 BILLION average video views a DAY (source: http://bit.ly/2OFrk8j).
- Snapchat (another mobile social network with a younger consumer demographic) is outpacing Facebook with their users generating 10 BILLION video views a DAY (source: http://bit.ly/2OKdGk9).
- Not bad when you consider Snapchat has just a fraction of Facebook's userbase, with 191 million daily mobile users.
- Instagram (also owned by Facebook) has also exploded since copying and implementing some of Snapchat's functionality and now has more than 500 million daily active users (source: http://bit.ly/2OLJDbT) with video watch time increasing 80% year on year (source: http://bit.ly/2OPQIYM).

Video

Don't think you should set up a broadcast centre or hire professional videographers to post video on social media.

This is a book all about mobile marketing, right? If you have a decent modern smartphone with a camera and video function, you should be good to go. If you don't have a smartphone and you're not sure which one to get, just go to Google and type something like 'best smartphone for under XXX'.

> Video content doesn't have to be super-slick high quality. A lot of the time 'amateur-looking' video has better engagement because it feels more authentic (because it is!), less staged and creates a deeper relationship with your audience.

- Publish your content at the most appropriate time during the day. Should you publish before 9am, at lunchtime, after 7pm? Some other time? You won't know in the beginning so just post a variety of different types of content (text, image, video) at various times during the day and then closely examine your social media account's analytics to see if that gives you any feedback on which content, which type of post and which time generates the best engagement with your audience.
- If you have more time than clients and customers then by all means handle everything yourself, but when the time comes, and your business begins to attract more and more clients and customers, don't waste a second and automate as much of the publishing process as possible.
- Yes, you need to curate, create and publish content, but you need to do it in the most time-efficient manner possible without sacrificing the quality of the service you provide to your customers. Outsource whatever content creation you can, when you can:
  - If it's an article you can hire a writer with knowledge in your field. Good writers cost around 7 cents a word, so a 1000-word article will be around $70.
  - If you going to publish inspirational quotes or tips in image form, there are thousands of graphic designers out there who will happily do this type of work for you.
  - If it's video, you can create it yourself with your phone or if it's something you can demonstrate on your computer you can use software like Camtasia Studio or Screenflow (Mac) to record your desktop and save it as a video to upload.
  - If it's a more professional type of video, there are tons of videographers as well as writers and graphic artists

in freelance marketplace sites like UpWork.com and Freelancer.com.

- Ideally, plan your content out a month in advance and if it's content to be outsourced have them create everything ahead of time, then use services like Buffer.com, Twitterfeed.com or Hootsuite.com to schedule your content to be posted to your accounts.

TIP *Before subscribing to a service, make sure they are able to do what you want them to do. Do you want them to auto-mate posting images or videos? Not all of them can. Do your research.*

Content ideas

Stuck on what to post? How about any of these?

- Look for birthdays of famous people who are related to your field of expertise. Are there any interesting facts about them you could publish?
- Is there an 'On this day in history ...' related to your field you could publish?
- Ask followers, subscribers or customers for questions and post an answer on a separate day.
- Post breaking news in your industry (find the best blogs in your industry and subscribe to their content using Feedly.com and make that your browser's homepage).

TIP *We've listed just a few ideas here. For more than 120 dif-ferent content ideas see: http://bit.ly/2OQxzWC.*

Where to publish

So we've covered what, why, when and how to publish content – now comes the where. Below I'm going to discuss the 'Big Three': Facebook, Twitter and LinkedIn but depending on your audience and the type of business you have, other mobile social networks might be a better fit. For instance:

- If you're an ecommerce operation servicing the teenager-early 20s demographic, you should also seriously consider Snapchat.
- If you have anything to do with fashion or health/fitness, start getting experience with Instagram.
- If you sell homewares, then Pinterest could well be your primary mobile social media network, even over Facebook. (Pinterest has a 70 per cent female demographic!)

Facebook

If you don't already have a Facebook Page for your business, you're missing out on possibly one of the best marketing opportunities you can get online. Your Facebook Page can potentially put your business in front of nearly a quarter of all the people on Earth – billions of people. Now maybe your company only serves your local community with a 20-mile radius. Well, because of the sheer numbers of people on Facebook, it's possible for you to market to the majority (if not all) of the targeted people in your service area.

And helpfully, Facebook has given you a tool which will tell you precisely how many people there are in your local area available to target on Facebook. It's called Audience Insights and you'll find it in your Facebook Ad account or you can go directly to it here (FB ad account required).

Audience Insights

- Personal Ad Account: https://www.facebook.com/ads/audience-insights
- Business Ad Account: https://business.facebook.com/ads/audience-insights

A Facebook Page can be created extremely quickly and is completely free to set up.

1 Go to https://www.facebook.com/pages/create/ to begin creating your page.
2 Select a category and Page name for your business.
3 Use your company logo or an image directly associated with your company as your Page's profile picture. The profile image dimensions at the time of writing are 180 × 180 pixels.
4 Write a short sentence or two describing your business (if you're stuck at this stage, open a new tab in your browser and have a look at what other businesses have written).
5 Create a web address for your page that is easy to remember and can be used in your marketing literature. This will help to promote your Facebook Page.
6 The last major thing is your Cover Image – that's the large 851 × 315 (at the time of writing) image at the top of your Facebook Page. This is one of the first things people will see when they view your Facebook Page so it's important to get this right.

TIP *Rather than list out dos and don'ts for creating a Facebook Page, HubSpot.com have a great article on the topic you can go through on their blog here: http://bit.ly/2R7vHdp.*

Once the Page is live, you can go in and add more optional information like a phone number, business address, mission statement and so on.

Once your Page is ready for visitors, you can initially reach out to friends, family and customers to 'Like' it and then in due course reach out to targeted prospects via natural organic reach and paid ads.

The type of content that tends to work best with Facebook is:

● Small-to-medium length text (no more than 500 words)
● Images
● Video (particularly FB Live)

If you intend to focus more on mobile marketing, I would concentrate more on image and video on Facebook.

Twitter

Twitter is a popular social media site that works in a similar way to SMS/Text messaging. Messages (called Tweets) are limited to 280 characters but you can also post images and videos up to 30 seconds long.

You decide on what shows up in your Twitter feed by the people and accounts you follow, like Facebook and most other social networks. You can 'Like', 'Favourite', 'Retweet' (share to your own followers) content as well as publicly and privately message (known as Direct Message or DM) other people.

Generally, both parties in a conversation would have to follow each other to be able to DM but you can turn on the ability to allow someone to DM you who hasn't followed you; perfect for companies to allow sales enquiries without the other party having to broadcast their interest to the world.

Twitter is an excellent way to keep up to date with current events and news, particularly when it comes to breaking news and interesting articles being published in real time.

Research has shown that 64 per cent of Twitter users are more likely to buy the products or brands they follow online (source: https://yhoo.it/2R9ZFgM) so whether you're servicing business-to-consumer (B2C) or business-to-business (B2B) you should seriously think about leveraging Twitter in your mobile social media marketing.

Setting up an account is quick, easy and free.

1 Go to http://twitter.com, click the 'Sign Up' button, fill in the email address you want to use and select a password. Then you'll be asked to select a Twitter username.
2 If you're publishing on behalf of your company, try to get your company's name as the username. With 350 million users there's a chance that it may not be available, so you'll need to improvise a little.
3 Once you've got a username you're happy with and that's available, click the 'Create My Account' button and it'll log

you in and you're ready to use Twitter. You cannot change the username later so make sure you're 100 per cent happy with it. NOTE: Double check the email address you use because Twitter will send you a verification email with a link inside it that you'll need to click to give you full access to all Twitter's functions.

4 Do the usual things, like adding a short benefit-driven bio and profile pictures (a company logo is fine) and you're good to go.

The type of content that tends to work best with Twitter is more newsy type content, links out to topic content or anything that's easily consumable.

LinkedIn

LinkedIn is a professional social network with over 590 million members. Since it's a professional network made up of entrepreneurs, business owners, executives and the 'C-Suite' (CEO, COO, CMO etc.), if you service businesses in any way, it makes sense for LinkedIn to be a foundation of your mobile social media plan.

If you don't already have a LinkedIn account, here's how to start:

1 Sign up for a personal account (you'll need one of these first before you can create a business one). Just go to http://www.linkedin.com, fill in the form and click the 'Join Now' button. You'll need to verify your email address so check your email and click the confirmation link in the email LinkedIn sends you.

2 After clicking the confirmation link you'll be taken back to LinkedIn where you can choose the type of account you need, based on what you primarily want to use LinkedIn for. There's the basic free account or you can select one of the premium offerings that give you more functionality. Pick the one you want then go to your Profile and begin to edit it putting in all your relevant information.

3 You'll see a field for entering your company's website – use the format http://www.yourwebsite.com. This will create a live link to your company, and any other members of your

staff on LinkedIn can also use this hyperlink to link back to your company's website.

TIP *Your industry field is searchable so think very carefully what you put in here. I'd advise doing some research into your competitors to see if a) they're on LinkedIn and b) what industry field they've entered. Choosing the right entry makes the difference between being seen or not.*

4 Once you've completed your personal profile, create a Company Page (like a Facebook Page) and fill that in with all the appropriate information.

LinkedIn is the same as any social media network. If you want to be seen, you must get involved. Download the app onto your phone and start getting out there. Connect with people you know and start building your network.

The best type of content to post on LinkedIn is informative and educational in nature. The type of content you can post includes:

- Medium to longer text (400+ words)
- Video
- PDFs (case studies, white papers etc.)

A great way to leverage LinkedIn is to look for relevant LinkedIn groups to join – be they related to your field of expertise, your location, a local Chamber of Commerce or something else.

Give help and advice where you can, share insights and just generally contribute. The exposure will help lead you to a bigger audience and eventually to make more contacts which in turn will increase the chance of obtaining new customers and clients.

TIP *There are lots of tutorials on how to use LinkedIn on their official YouTube Channel here: https://www.youtube.com/user/LinkedIn.*

Summary

Just as the world is going mobile, so it is going social. To get mobile traffic, you need to be active on all the major social networks as much as possible. This helps build both your brand and your relationships with your clients/customers.

Each social network has its own special rules and ways to sign up correctly that I don't possibly have room for in a summary, but they are all mostly common sense (as far as the web is concerned). Just to be safe, be sure to bookmark and/or highlight the sections that deal with the social networks that you will be signing up on.

But there is one thing all social networks want and that is content. To do anything on these sites and drive traffic to you, you need to be producing content that gets the 'click'.

Make sure your content is 'on topic' and relevant to your business. Be down to earth and fun as much as possible – avoid being too formal. Write high-quality content and post cool relevant pictures, but most of all try and produce good videos. Videos tend to get great traction and can lead to serious

SUNDAY MONDAY TUESDAY WEDNESDAY THURSDAY FRIDAY SATURDAY

traffic from YouTube and other social networks if done right.

Depending on your niche and/or business, be sure to have a plan to produce content. Whether it is you, an employee or some other freelancer creating it, make sure it is high quality content and being created consistently.

In this chapter we looked at a general overview of the 'Big Three' social networks and at some of the pluses and minuses with each, but really you should be on all of them. Later we will look at tools you can use to cut down on the time spent managing these networks – so never fear.

Fact-check (answers at the back)

1. Why are we talking about social media in a mobile marketing book?
a) Because this book has seven chapters and this fills one of them. ❑
b) Social media is cool and hip. ❑
c) Mobile users are all over social media. ❑
d) I felt like it, what is your problem? ❑

2. Social media benefits:
a) Your brand ❑
b) Your visibility ❑
c) Your relationships with your customers. ❑
d) All of the above ❑

3. What percentage of people said a company's social media profile influenced their decision to buy once (positively or negatively):
a) 50% ❑
b) 25% ❑
c) 78% ❑
d) 85% ❑
e) 56% ❑

4. Businesses don't use social media to make decisions so B2B companies don't need to be on social media.
a) True ❑
b) False ❑

5. You need good _____ to succeed on social media.
a) Cat photos ❑
b) Witty comments on current events ❑
c) Random shared items ❑
d) Content (video or other) ❑
e) None of the above. ❑

6. The best kind of content currently in most niches is:
a) Written articles ❑
b) Video ❑
c) Photos ❑
d) Plain comments ❑

7. The demographic of Pinterest is:
a) 30% female ❑
b) 55% female ❑
c) 70% female ❑
d) 85% female ❑

8. If you are targeting teenagers/20-somethings then you should be on:
a) Twitter ❑
b) Instagram ❑
c) Snapchat ❑
d) Facebook ❑
e) Other ❑

9. LinkedIn should be your main social network if:
a) You do cat videos ❑
b) You are a B2B company ❑
c) You are a B2C company ❑
d) You are a videographer ❑

10. Twitter is best for:
a) News ❑
b) Posting content ❑
c) Engaging with followers ❑
d) All of the above ❑

WEDNESDAY

Mobile
pay-per-
click (PPC)
marketing

Today we are going to discuss the #1 traffic methodology that every mobile marketer needs to master and that is pay-per-click (PPC) marketing.

SEO and social media are great ways to generate traffic and build brand awareness but if you don't have your sales processes working and optimized, all that traffic will be wasted.

So how do you figure out your sales processes? Using paid traffic to jump start visitors to your website as quickly as possible to test, tweak and improve your sales and conversion processes. Then when you think you've got something working that's profitable, you start ramping up your social media and organic search campaigns.

If there's one thing I want you to take away from reading this book, it's this: don't choose between paid traffic, or social media marketing or SEO – they all work in synergy **together**.

DISCLAIMER: Just so we're clear I'm not saying that you're guaranteed to make money when you use PPC traffic. No traffic, whether paid, social or organic, is a 'magic money bullet'. What PPC traffic **can** do is generate traffic quickly to your website for you to work with.

I don't know anything about you, your skill set or your offers, so like any other aspect of business, it requires spending time learning how to do it, which may mean (shudder) math and some common sense to be able to make sense of the numbers and apply what you learn from them.

That legal stuff out of the way, let's talk about the state of the mobile PPC market first and then get into how to do it right.

Mobile PPC in a nutshell

Firstly, some context ...

- There are 6.8 billion people on the planet. 5.1 billion of them own a cell phone, but only 4.2 billion own a toothbrush. (Source: Mobile Marketing Association Asia)
- It takes 26 hours for the average person to report a lost wallet. It takes 68 *minutes* for them to report a lost phone. (Source: Unisys)
- Over 52% of all website traffic worldwide is generated by mobile phones (source: Statista).

What does all this mean? People value their mobile phones seemingly more than their teeth or their money. But seriously, now mobile *is* the internet and because there are that many people accessible, mobile paid traffic is a lot cheaper and plentiful than desktop traffic.

You also tend to find with mobile ad networks you have more ways to drill down and optimize your traffic than you do with desktop traffic. For example, some networks will let you filter and optimize your ad campaigns by:

- **Geo:** a specific town, city, state
- **Device:** only showing ads on a certain make or model or type of device
- **Carrier:** want to only show your ad to people on AT&T or Verizon? No problem
- **OS:** you can specify to only show ads to people running iOS, Android etc.
- **Connection:** you can limit your ads to only show to those people on a 3G or 4G/LTE connection but no Wi-Fi.

And some networks have even more ways to filter.

Like desktop traffic, not all sources generate the same quality of visitor.

There are also different types of traffic you can purchase, especially with mobile. Of course, there is Google AdWords, one of the Tier 1 networks where you can place ads to show up on certain searches and you can also advertise within mobile apps that allow ads to be shown within them.

There's YouTube, where you can have ads running before and during a video being played (and on desktop beside the ad on the page).

Then there is Facebook, which is Google's main competitor in the mobile PPC space which can show ads before and during videos, in your newsfeed and within Instagram which it also owns. For me personally, I prefer Facebook's targeting system (which we'll get into later today) and the amount of targetable data it has about users is amazing.

Then there are the smaller Tier 1 players like Yahoo and Bing PPC, which operate in a similar way to Google with much less advertising inventory, but can generate high quality conversions depending on your offer, of course.

And there are hundreds of other smaller networks, some offering the same type of traffic, others offering completely different types of traffic then the Tier 1s. For example, there are 'pop networks' where traffic is generated from a pop-under

or a pop-up. A website owner signs up and places the pop-up/
-under code on their website and that website is then added to
the network's inventory as a place to run ads.

A business owner can target categories of websites to run
ads on with each website showing a pop-up/-under with the
business's ad on it. The website owner gets paid a few cents
per pop-up and the business owner is charged per pop shown.

Then there are 'redirect networks'. People and companies
will buy expired domain names and sell access to those
domains to redirect networks who will categorize them and
sell access to businesses.

*To get an idea of just how much of this redirect traffic is
out there, check out a mobile network called ZeroPark and
go to their 'Network Volume' page here: https://zeropark.
com/volume. Play around with those settings and prepared
to be amazed at how much traffic there is and how little
it costs.*

So how does mobile PPC marketing work? There are two main
types of PPC – keyword related and demographically related.

Google

Keyword related is how Google does it in their Search Network.
You bid on which keywords (search terms) your ad will show up
above the organic search results and you pay $x.xx or just $.xx
every time your advert is clicked.

You can find out the average cost per click (CPC) for each
keyword using either the Google Keyword Planner or Google's
Traffic Estimator tool (accessible only from within an AdWords
account).

The price you pay is a combination of the amount of competition
for the keyword and how popular your ad is. The more times
your ad is clicked in your PPC campaign, Google rewards you
by ever-so-slowly nudging you up the paid ad rankings.

So, if your ad was initially placed fourth and ended up getting
more clicks than the third, second and first place ads, it's

possible that your ad will jump the queue into first place and you'll still be paying the same amount as you were when you were in fourth place.

Once again, Google rewards relevancy with ranking, and because ads in first place generally get more clicks than lower-positioned ads (assuming it does get the clicks), you'll end up sending more traffic to your website at a lower cost than your competitors!

Google generally has a higher quality of conversion over Facebook because you're able to target those exhibiting an intent to purchase, for example if they're searching for the best type of business near them or a specific product.

Google/AdMob in-app advertising 'network'

In 2006 the AdMob network launched offering advertising within mobile apps and games and was wildly successful. Three years later, they were bought by Google and their network was integrated (assimilated?) into Google's.

You can also use banner images and even advertise using video ads within mobile apps and games as well as showing ads within the regular Google Search results but only from a mobile device.

So for example, if you have a game that you think will appeal to the Candy Crush Saga users on Android, you can bid for your ad to appear at the top of Google search results for people who have downloaded Candy Crush Saga on their Android phone.

Second, you don't bid on keywords shown up from a search; instead you bid to show your ad on pages Google deems relevant to a keyword.

You can pay CPM (Cost Per Mille, the cost per 1,000 impressions. So when Google shows your ad 1,000 times, you pay $x.xx regardless of whether your ads are clicked or not) or even CPA (Cost Per Action) so if you're advertising an app or a game you only pay if it's downloaded.

Facebook mobile ads

Facebook does both PPC and CPM but they are demographic-based which means that instead of targeting what people are searching for, you can target people per *who* they are, for instance the things they like, their occupation, their age, their sex and so on.

Although you can do this type of demographic targeting in Google, it's nowhere as detailed as it is in Facebook, because Google simply doesn't have the data which is likely why Google+ was created originally before it was shut down.

Ad volume is massive (2.19 billion available global Facebook users and growing) and the pricing is extremely good.

The one thing you need to remember about Facebook ads is that they are *interrupting* a person's usage on the platform, just the same as commercials on TV and radio. They aren't explicitly searching for information about a product or service so even with the 100% accurate customer targeting your campaigns aren't going to have as high a conversion rate as keyword-based ones like in Google.

But don't worry, once you have your campaigns dialled in they can be *extremely* profitable regardless.

Bing/Yahoo mobile ads

Bing/Yahoo ads follow similar rules to Google, and even though they have a much lower ad inventory than Google, Yahoo and Facebook in many cases can generate higher quality conversions (especially if your ideal customer is older and less tech-savvy) was OK.

If you're just starting out with mobile PPC, I suggest you focus your efforts on Facebook and Google so you can reach the most people the fastest.

Pros and cons of mobile PPC

Pros

You know that people are at least vaguely interested in what you have – they went and clicked your ad so they must be at least curious to see what is on the other side (if you wrote your ad right that is, more on this later).

You can really focus down to the very nitty-gritty for your visitors.

If you want people from North Dakota who like bubble gum and rock'n'roll, you can find them with Facebook (not quite in such detail as with Google, though you could find people that are searching for terms around rock'n'roll or bubble gum, just not both in the same campaign).

You can say with (almost) certainty that you will get traffic.

When they're on the ball, both Google and Facebook can approve an ad very quickly – I've personally had ads approved and live in less than 10 minutes before but it's normally within an hour or two.

Cons

Costs per click (CPC) are gradually rising and can be unnaturally high unless you do proper research, choose your correct keywords or demographics and point ads to a specific page on your site, not your homepage.

Both Facebook and Google are now public companies, answering to shareholders and having to go out of their way to make sure that they are profitable – and that means extracting as much money as possible from advertisers.

CPCs can range anywhere from 5 cents to $50 a click and sometimes more (it depends on the market and keywords being bid on). So you really have to do your research into every word or interest you are bidding on to make sure that you are getting the best bang for your buck. Even this can get expensive really fast.

Luckily, both Google and Facebook allow you to set daily budgets that you cannot go over, so you shouldn't have to sell a kidney or your firstborn to pay your PPC bill. But that daily limit needs to consider the number of clicks you want; clicks sending people to your website.

Killer tip

When running a PPC campaign, instead of setting a daily budget, set a lifetime budget for the same amount over a set period of days. So for example, instead of setting a daily budget of $20/day, set it for $600 for the month. This gives the ad network's systems time to figure out how best to optimize your campaigns. This trick works especially well with Facebook.

You need to keep in your mind though that you should aim to generate at least 200 visitors a day to your test URLs so you can be reasonably sure which item you're testing is the winner. Here's a great online calculator that will help to tell you whether your testing results are statistically significant: http://bit.ly/2R06PnZ.

Also, make sure that you set your budget high enough so you can get at least 200 daily visitors.

Research and tracking

Some keywords may be expensive but might end up converting less well than other cheaper keywords for you or vice-versa. So you need to do research combined with a lot of tracking. Tracking is where you see where the traffic is coming from and how well it converts (how much people do what you want them to). Compare the keywords to other keywords and narrow down exactly what you need. Both Facebook and Google have free tools that will allow you to track sales, leads or other outcomes and so on.

Mobile PPC advertising strategies

So now you have a focus, how will you set up your campaigns? First you need to watch the relevant tutorial videos provided by Google and Bing to show you the mechanics of creating campaigns and ad groups:

- http://google.com/adwords/onlineclassroom
- http://advertise.bingads.microsoft.com/en-us/new-to-search-marketing (click the Getting Started tab on Bing for even more video tutorials).

Then you can look at structuring your PPC ad campaigns on the Google and Bing search networks. The most common way is to use the 'long-tail keyword' approach by creating multiple ad groups, each revolving around a main root keyword and having similar keywords in the same group.

If we go back to the dog grooming example we used previously, and I type in the keyword 'dog grooming' into Google's Keyword Tool, I get a series of keywords all grouped together by theme like:

KIT:

- dog grooming kit
- dog grooming kits
- grooming kits for dogs
- dog grooming kits for sale
- dog grooming starter kit

TUBS:

- dog grooming tubs
- dog grooming tub
- dog grooming bath tubs
- dog wash tub
- dog grooming tubs for sale
- used dog grooming tubs
- dog bath tub
- dog grooming baths

CLIPPERS:

- dog grooming clippers
- best dog grooming clippers
- dog grooming clippers reviews
- Wahl dog grooming clippers
- clippers for dog grooming
- dog grooming clippers Australia
- best dog clippers
- dog grooming clippers for sale
- clippers dog grooming
- dog grooming clippers UK

Plus a lot more ...

Once you've selected the keywords and ad groups you want to use, you can transfer them into an existing campaign in your Google AdWords account (if you're already logged in) with a couple of mouse clicks by selecting the 'Add To Account' button.

Bing isn't quite as refined a process as Google's so what I generally do is to use the exact same keywords and ad grouping in Bing. If you use the free Google AdWords Editor and Bing Ads Editor software programs, you can easily export your Google campaigns and import them into Bing quickly and easily. Just search in Google for 'Bing Ads Editor' and 'Google AdWords Editor' to get the download links for your country.

Some quick dos and don'ts

Do

- Set a budget you can afford even if it doesn't convert at all.
- Test many different headlines and body texts of your ads and see which work out and which don't.
- Try and focus down on the exact keywords that you want to get clicks on. The more specific, the cheaper and more effective the click becomes.
- Wherever possible, point an ad to a page on your website that is directly related to your ad. Do not just send visitors to your website's homepage.
- If possible, offer something on the webpage you're sending people to in exchange for an email address or phone number. That will let you continue to follow up for free to maximize your chance at making a sale.
- Read Google and Facebook's ad policies carefully before you place a single ad so you know what you can and can't do (and the products you can't advertise) on their networks.

Don't

● Try to send visitors to a page where you try and get them to click another ad. This is known as 'arbitrage' and will result in having your account banned.

● Make low-quality landing pages that are not directly relevant to the ad text. For more information on best practices for landing pages, refer to this guide by Google: http://bit.ly/ReH2nd.

● Write headlines or body text just to get clicks. Clicks are not the point – the point is to get people who are already interested in what they will get on the other side.

PPC strategies for Facebook

As mentioned before, Facebook is a different beast because there are no keywords as such to bid to show your ad for. Instead, you need to target people interested in related subjects, located in a certain geographic area, by the college or university they went to, their sex or any other combinations of demographic information.

Based upon my own experiences with Facebook PPC, here's how I recommend you structure your campaigns:

Where possible, link your ads to a post on a Facebook Page. Facebook doesn't like it when you take users directly outside of Facebook. In my tests, the costs per click of my campaigns *halved* when I sent people to a Facebook Page instead of an external URL.

If you intend to run a PPC campaign to generate Likes for your company's Facebook Page, also consider creating a Facebook Page for a celebrity or subject that has a broad appeal and is somehow related to your product or service and then running a PPC campaign to generate Likes for that page too.

For example, if you are a weight loss consultant who specializes in helping women lose weight and get fit, you might create a Facebook Page around a female celebrity who has successfully lost weight and now looks great, for instance

Jennifer Hudson if you're in the USA or maybe Davina McCall if you're in the UK.

Piggy-backing on a celebrity or broad subject like 'weight loss' should make it easier to generate Likes for that page, targeting people using your criteria (local area, sex, age, etc.) and then you can send occasional 'promoted posts' to your fans with special offers on your company Facebook Page.

> ## Something to ponder
>
> If you have a lot of fans/Likes for your broad subject Facebook page, you might be able to sell 'promoted posts' to other companies not in direct competition with you, generating another revenue stream. Just a thought ...
>
> Oh and BTW, would you be interested in a free resource where you can find around 20,000 examples of Facebook ads categorized by Placements, Industries, Objectives and Type? Here you go: http://bit.ly/2OdgmHz.
>
> You're welcome!

Retargeting

Retargeting is a technique that few businesses know how to do, which is a shame because it is phenomenally powerful.

You as the website owner place a special code on all the pages on your website (sometimes called a retargeting pixel or tracking pixel). When someone visits any page on your website, a small text file called a cookie is placed on their computer containing various bits of anonymous information including a unique identifier.

(There's no need to worry about cookies, they're not viruses or anything like that.)

The traffic network is then able to track certain activities on your website like the webpages they view, for how long, if they place an order – things like that.

Over time and using this ever-increasing datastore, you're able to build audiences of people who have performed certain actions on your website and run ads only to them.

Here are a couple of examples to get you thinking just how powerful this can be:

1 What if you ran a retargeting ad only to people who visited a specific product on your site <u>and</u> abandoned your order page without buying ... and offered them a 10% discount code if they order within 24 hours?
2 What if you ran a retargeting ad only to people who bought your bronze level package within the last 7 days with an offer to get a free 1 hour consulting call worth $xxx if they upgrade to your Silver level package?
3 What if you ran a retargeting ad only to people who bought a specific item (like a formal shirt) and offered a tie and cufflinks set to go with it?

How powerful and effective do you think those types of targeted campaigns would be?

You can also use retargeting to build brand awareness to your audience, seeming like you're everywhere. For instance, if you put a retargeting pixel on your blog you can run a campaign targeting websites in a similar category so when your visitors leave and visit these websites, they'll keep seeing your ads – literally following them around. This can be on everywhere from other Google sites, on Facebook, as well as Yahoo.

As 99 per cent of those people that visit your website through social media/SEO and PPC will not buy right away, this means that those potential customers will now have a chance to come back when they are ready to buy without having to remember your website's name and URL.

Your visitors will suddenly start seeing your ads at their favourite websites and the sites they visit every day like Facebook, causing them to slowly but surely begin to trust you more and more and see you as an authority if only because they saw your ad on the *New York Times* website.

The services I use for this are:

● http://adroll.com
● http://perfectaudience.com
● http://sitescout.com

Most major traffic platforms also offer retargeting within their own platform. Facebook, Instagram and Twitter offer retargeting within themselves and Google offers a service called Remarketing (it's the same thing). All offer simple and elegant solutions and reach a *lot* of users around the world.

YouTube Ads and Facebook

YouTube is the second biggest search engine in the world and it is totally worth your time to create videos to get traffic. Now though, with their pay-per-view program, they have become even more potent.

Say you create a video but you are wondering if it converts real fast? Spend $20 and get a bunch of views to it and see! Out of those views, how many clicked through to your page? How many of those became customers?

At this point you might want to optimize it more and edit it a bit. With YouTube's average view time, you can see where people start to drop off and it might give you an idea of what to change. Or it might make sense to leave the ad up and continue to pay for views. Otherwise, if it still converts and retains your audience but not enough to make sense continuing the ads, just keep it up on YouTube and get natural views.

Either way it is a win–win–win for you by saving time and helping you improve at the same time. Once you get a few good videos converting well on YouTube, consider setting up a campaign on Facebook as well, driving dirt-cheap clicks to these. This way you can get multiple uses out of your successes.

Summary

Sorry this was so long today, but we did have a lot to cover.

To sum it all up, there are two major players in PPC (pay-per-click) ads: Facebook and Google (with YouTube a close third). These two are where you should do your tests first – before going anywhere else – and are the easiest to get up and running and get traffic fast. The point at the beginning is risk small, and only lose small. But see what happens and learn big from it.

Don't expect to make any sales at first. Aim to learn. With that in mind, be sure you know what you want the person on the other end to do. Do you want them to give you their email? Or some other info?

There are no hard and fast rules, only guidelines. What works for me and my niche might not work for yours.

Follow my guidelines today and you should be on the right track from the start. Then once you have started to be profitable in one PPC network (Google or Facebook), you can branch out to YouTube and/or other

SUNDAY MONDAY TUESDAY WEDNESDAY THURSDAY FRIDAY SATURDAY advertisers like Yahoo. Try to adapt what you learned from before to the new medium and scale from there.

After this consider retargeting. This is a great way to get all those misses to become hits. After all, in a good campaign, literally 95 per cent can leave and not do anything and it could be considered a success. With re-targeting you can cheaply follow up with those people and add a few more percentage points to the board over time.

So I hope you learned something great today! On to the next day ...

Fact-check (answers at the back)

1. PPC stands for:
a) Perfectly politically correct ❑
b) Payment potentially considered ❑
c) Pay-per-click ❑
d) Panning people consolidated ❑

2. The main PPC giants are:
a) Facebook ❑
b) Google ❑
c) YouTube ❑
d) Bing ❑
e) Everybody else ❑
f) a, b, and c ❑

3. Be sure and place a daily limit based on:
a) How much you expect to make ❑
b) The size of the market ❑
c) How much you can afford to completely lose ❑

4. CPM stands for:
a) Cost per million impressions ❑
b) Clicks per month ❑
c) Cost per mille (1000) impressions ❑

5. Your home page:
a) Is a good page to use PPC to get clients ❑
b) Is a bad page to drive PPC traffic to ❑
c) May or may not work ❑

6. When you do PPC, it is good to have the focus of those clicks to be:
a) Four different options ❑
b) Three different options ❑
c) Two different options ❑
d) One measurable thing that you want them to do ❑

7. Before you start some PPC campaigns, you should know:
a) Your lifetime client value ❑
b) How much you are willing to spend ❑
c) What you want the click to do ❑
d) What you will do with the information you are going to glean ❑
e) All of the above ❑

8. In your PPC campaign always try to:
a) Make sales for your efforts ❑
b) Learn everything about your clients for your efforts ❑
c) Get at least an email address for your efforts ❑

9. Landing pages are:
a) Where the potential client 'lands' after clicking on your ad ❑
b) One-page sites that you clients want to visit ❑
c) Only for users of private planes ❑

10. Retargeting ads means:
a) Someone visiting your website will now see targeted ads on other pages. ❑
b) You will know where they live to set up your sniper nest. ❑
c) You can now find out everything about this person. ❑
d) b and c ❑

THURSDAY

Mobile apps for small business

It's safe to say that one of the reasons (if not the main reason) that smartphones have become so successful in recent years is because of the apps that run on them.

Without the apps, you've got a nice touchscreen phone that can play music and surf the web, which is all great and everything ... but there's nothing particularly special about that.

There were quite a few smartphones before the iPhone but the apps on them were basic, slow and not particularly fun or easy to use. Email was generally only available if your phone was connected to your company's servers and the internet was a 'baby' version.

And then in 2007 the iPhone was released which triggered a seismic shift in the entire mobile phone industry. With the iPhone, you had an operating system based on their desktop OSX, a large (then!) touchscreen that you didn't need a stylus to use, proper email that would work with any normal email system and a web browser that enabled you to surf the full web.

In other words, a true personal computer that fits in your pocket.

At the core, fully-featured, desktop-class software applications that are easier and cheaper to develop, putting them within reach of any size of business.

Today, I'm going to go through exactly what an app is, why you might think about having an app developed, how to get one created and how you can make one yourself, whether to give it away or charge for it and how to get your target audience to download it.

What exactly is an 'app'?

An app is just a nickname for a 'program application' that is designed to perform certain functions on your phone, tablet, computer or TV (yes TVs have them now too).

They do all kinds of things. I have one that checks my blood pressure and counts my steps (I am seriously inactive, I need to work out). There's Skype so I can audio/video call and send messages to annoy my staff (they love me really). I have an app that will allow me to connect my phone to the PC in my office and control it like I was sitting in front of it from anywhere in the world with an internet connection.

I can search for houses for sale, get sports results, shop online, buy domain names, check the weather, stream millions of songs into my phone, watch TV and movies, tune my guitar, work out my taxes, learn how to draw, read a magazine, navigate from anywhere to anywhere else in the world. Get from place to place with a map app.

You can play a piano on your phone, track your investments, help you get focused (which is getting harder to do because, you know ... I have dozens of apps on my phone). Not to mention some of the weirdest apps you can imagine serving no purpose, like an app that add cats shooting laser beams out of its eyes to your own photos. I'm not kidding: https://apple.co/2R8nHbY.

And the list goes on and on. It is absolutely nuts. With 3.3 million apps in the Google Play Store and 3.8 million in Apple's App Store it's safe to say that if you can think of it (and maybe even if you can't think of it) there is probably 'an app for that'.

Why should *I* consider creating an app?

- In the USA, 90 per cent of time on a mobile phone is spent within apps (source: Yahoo Flurry Analytics).
- For retailers, conversions are 3x higher from an app than a mobile website (source: Criteo https://mklnd.com/2yrzl6t).

Smartphone users are already preconditioned to download and use apps so this isn't anything they're not already doing and require 'training' for. A custom mobile app specifically designed for your business can give your customer instant access to you, your product and services and any special 'app only' offers you choose to run.

Apps can leverage the incredible marketing power of push notifications, the little message alert boxes that ding up telling you to do something. And you know what? They work like gangbusters, boosting app engagement as much as 88 per cent when used appropriately (e.g. a news site can push more notifications about current events than a retailer without it looking spammy).

With 50 billion in-phone push notifications sent to 900 million mobile users worldwide just in the first half of 2018 (source: http://bit.ly/2yvVReG) and the functionality now being available in the popular desktop and mobile web browsers, maybe this is a tactic you could also consider?

WOW! I definitely need an app for my business!

Hold on there, tiger! First you need to make the business case for it.

If you're a retailer or service provider able to take orders and clients from anywhere in the country (or the world) then an app could be a good way to increase your company's visibility and begin to build a great relationship with potential customers and clients.

If you're a business targeting a local geographic area, it's a little trickier because you have much lower number of potential customers and clients so it will all depend on the profit margins you're operating with and the development cost for the app. Let's consider some examples.

Example 1

You're a cosmetic dental surgeon with an average customer value of $10,000 with approx. 40 per cent profit ($4,000).

Let's assume women aged 30+ in California are your potential target audience (at least 9 million people according to Facebook) and your app costs $5,000 to create.

You only need two new clients *ever* to come through the app for it to more than pay for itself.

Example 2

Now let's say you own a stationery store servicing downtown San Diego's 37,000 residents.

Your average order is $75 with a 30 per cent profit margin ($22.50) and your app costs the same $5,000 to build. You are going to need 222 new customers spending at least $75 to recoup your app's investment.

I've plucked figures out of thin air here, so your app may cost a lot more or less to create, depending on how complex or not it is but you see where I'm going with this. I'll share some tools and resources you can use in a while to dramatically reduce development time and costs but my advice is, do your figure work before you commit to having an app developed.

If an app looks like it's practically not feasible to be developed, don't worry – here's another approach that's almost as valuable to your customers and clients and has the advantage of being faster to get up and running. Why not go through Apple's and Google's app stores and see if there are *related* apps on there already you could recommend to make your clients'/customers' lives better? For example if you're an accountant, find the best tax calculator or accounting app. If you're a personal trainer, find an exercise app that's good and offer a meal plan, nutrition tips or advice for perfect form.

You get the drift ...

You could:

- Write a blogpost with screenshots
- Format the blogpost as a PDF report instead and give it away in exchange for their email address
- Record a tutorial video showing how to use it.

Then either write a post about it linking to your website on Facebook and run ads to it or if you have a customer email list you can contact them directly and send them a link to the information.

I've decided to have an app created – what's next?

First you need to figure out what your app is going to do and how much you're going to spend on it (see the examples above), the first having a direct effect on the latter.

Whatever you decide it needs to be genuinely useful *and* act as a direct marketing tool to generate revenue for your business. It should offer an easy way for customers to get in touch with you and shouldn't contain any extra frippery. You don't need to give your app a flashlight or a compass unless you're a survival training consultant. For instance, if you're a dog groomer, how about a simple appointment setting and reminder app that would automatically schedule customers to come by every x weeks or whatever frequency the user would set? Maybe there could be a 'Pooch Panic Button' for when Trixie runs off through a muddy puddle and needs a top-to-tail emergency grooming?

Another use could be for a rewards programme for your business? Every time a customer spends a certain amount, they earn a 'stamp' on their digital card. Once they have collected a certain number of stamps you can offer a free extra 'something' or a percentage off any order over a certain amount. This is a great idea, because it gives the customer a reason to keep the app on their phone (i.e. it saves them money). Which brings me to the second point ...

They need to be customized to the customer.

If you have a business that has a lot of options or is a more 'on demand' type business, then you might consider an app.

For instance, let's say you are a plant hire company (the big machinery type of plant, not the floral kind) and most of your customers are construction firms. What would be genuinely useful to a construction site manager?

In large-scale construction, the harsh reality is that time really is money for a CSM, especially if they're operating on a hard deadline with a hard budget. What about developing an app that interfaces with your stock control system showing the availability and pricing of all your various equipment? A site manager could then hire whatever machinery they need for however long they need it *on their phone* standing in the middle of a building site without having to waste time trying to get someone on the phone to find out what's available.

Or maybe you're a vehicle recovery company and you want a super-simple app your customers could use to alert you that they need your help. Your app could be as simple as hitting a big-red virtual 'Panic Button' that hooks into Google/Apple Maps and texts the person's GPS co-ordinates along with their name, phone number, vehicle make/model and registration (pre-entered by the phone owner in the app's Settings section) to a dedicated phone number.

If this type of app would be great for your company but works out to be a little pricey, why not see if similar companies in other locations around the country who aren't in direct competition with you would be interested in splitting the development cost?

The app would simply contact the nearest recovery company when the button was pressed. Or you could always have the app created and then license it to similar companies in different areas and turn the app into a new revenue stream for your business? Have a think about the ways you could share the costs and the benefits with others.

Other uses for apps

An incident happened the other day that is the perfect example of how apps can be used in business. At an upscale clothing store my wife wanted to try something on, but we couldn't find her size. We showed it to the lady there and she whipped out her mobile phone and scanned the barcode and told us they had her size and to give her a few moments so she could get it.

How awesome is that?

Instead of having to spend thousands for *each* store for barcoding equipment that only has one use, they only had to pay once to come up with an app that does that and the staff just need to download an app to their phone.

Maybe this could also be an option for you and your business? Could you possibly come up with an app that would help your employees do their job faster, easier or better? Maybe they work in a factory and need to be reminded to do certain things on time. Maybe you could get an app made that reminds them exactly what to do and when to do it.

Ask your employees what they have the most problem with during the working day that might be solved with an app? They might have ideas that you never dreamed about.

How much does it cost?

This might be the defining factor for you that determines whether you develop an app or not. You will need to consider the following factors:

- **Obvious:** The more complex the functionality, the longer it will take to create and therefore the more it will cost.
- **Not-so-obvious:** *How* it is coded will affect the cost.

There are three general types of apps: native, hybrid and web.

Native apps

These are apps that have been coded using the specific programming tools for the operating system, will have direct access to all the various functionality and systems that the phone will allow and because of their specific programming (all things being equal) native apps will run faster than other types of apps.

Native apps coded for Apple's iOS will not work on the Android operating system and vice versa.

Hybrid apps

These are apps that have been written in such a way to perform as closely as possible to a native app but that can be run on the major mobile operating systems. This is generally referred to as WORA (Write Once, Run Anywhere).

WORA development systems are getting more and more sophisticated every year and their functionalities are getting larger and larger as other programmers donate modules they've created to perform specific tasks back to the relevant communities – making each generation of hybrid apps easier and quicker (and therefore cheaper!) to develop.

Popular WORA development systems are: React Native, Ionic, PhoneGap, Xamarin and Titanium.

Web apps

Web apps are exactly what they sound like – in essence mobile websites wrapped in a native programming 'shell' to make them appear more like an app on the phone.

However, the difference and distance between web apps and hybrid apps is decreasing thanks to the improvements to HTML webpage markup and Javascript.

The latest HTML standard for webpages, HTML5, is able to do a lot of very clever and powerful things that only a few years ago would be impossible with the HTML available at the time. When HTML5 is paired with Javascript frameworks like Angular.js (used by Google), React.js (used by Facebook and Instagram), Meteor.js and others you end up with incredibly powerful, incredibly fast web-based applications that are quick to create.

If your app idea is a simple one, it's possible that a web-based app could be enough to do the job.

Creating the app

It goes without saying that as a business owner, unless you have a serious geek itch that needs scratching you should absolutely get someone else to create the app.

If you're not into hiring and firing and all that and you just want to talk with someone and they handle all of that, I would check out here for ideas on price: https://www.otreva.com/calculator/.

As you will note it is quite a bit different between the two prices. Don't take this as the final word though. Shop around; you may find someone else willing to do your idea within your budget.

If your app idea is quite simple, there are marketplaces where you can buy pre-built apps that can be quickly and easily customized for your business.

Here's a great article showing nine places where you can buy pre-built app code: http://bit.ly/2R4jQg9.

If you see an app there that doesn't quite do what you want, send a message to the developer to see what they can do.

To reduce the costs even more, you can hire programmers outside of your country. Programmers in the old Eastern Bloc countries, the Philippines, India and Pakistan are a lot cheaper than those in the West and just as capable.

In all my books I continually reference the freelancer marketplaces like UpWork.com, eLance.com, EasyOutsource.com and Guru.com where you submit your app's requirements and have programmers bid against each other to land the job.

When you write your app's project description, you need to go into as much detail as possible, being as specific as you can be when describing how each part of it should work. The best place to find examples of plain English project specification documents is on the freelancing websites I mentioned earlier.

Once you've printed out a few and looked at them it becomes easy to figure out the sort of information that a developer is going to require.

If you don't know the answer to something like 'What programming language do you want the app coded in?' tell them straight that you don't know, what do they recommend and most importantly WHY!

If they say '… because that's the coding language I work in!' that's not a good enough reason. Regardless of the answers they give, probe them … ask them why this way and not that.

Doing this will save you a lot of time and money from hiring the wrong person for the job and help to eliminate confusion between you and the programmer who ends up building your app.

If your time is valuable, you can of course also hire someone to find and hire the right programmer for the task. You can also find these people on the freelancer websites. If you have the budget, you can also hire a project manager for a fixed amount of time to make sure everything runs smoothly and just to keep you up to date with a daily email or 15-minute chat going over progress. There are plenty of project managers who've dealt with mobile app creation on the freelancer websites.

Do it yourself

If you don't think your app idea would require complicated programming, you might be able to build your app yourself using one of the latest generation 'drag-n-drop' app building tools.

Obviously, these types of apps aren't as fully-featured as something that has been custom-coded by a developer but it might be worth a look at some of these 'newbie-friendly' tools to see what's possible. If this doesn't work out, you can always contact a developer.

If you do decide to do it yourself, here are a few links where you can find a list of useful tools:

- Zapable: http://zapable.com
- Good Barber: http://www.goodbarber.com
- Shout Em: http://shoutem.com
- App Yourself: http://appyourself.net
- Como: http://como.com

Getting your app in Apple's App Store and Google's Play Store

Even if you aren't creating an app to give away or sell to the whole world, your best chance of getting it into the hands of your customers and clients is to make it available to download from the official Apple App Store and Google Play Store. This is because:

- Apple and Google review every app that's submitted for any potential behaviour that could be deemed 'unsavoury' and a potential security risk.
- Both Apple and Google require ID and other types of documentation proof just to set up a developer account so there's always a way to track down the creator of a malicious app.
- Just making it available to download from your own website will require you to spend a lot of money upgrading the security of your servers to minimize the ability of hackers somehow getting in and compromising your app and then getting hold of your customers' and clients' personal information.

Therefore, if you can direct people to search for your app's name on the App Store or Google Play Store, or give them a direct download link to it, it reassures them that your app is legit and will save you a ton of headaches trying to do it yourself.

Rather than write out everything you need to know, here are a couple of videos walking you through the process.

- https://developer.apple.com/programs/enroll/ ←= Apple's Developer Program
- https://developer.android.com/distribute/ ←= Google's Android Developer Program

Promoting your app

In my opinion, this is the easiest bit, but your approach should be different for existing and new customers:

Existing customers

This can be as simple as setting up a page on your website that links where visitors can download your app from Apple's App Store and/or the Google Play Store. Something like:
http://www.yourdomain.com/downloadapp
And then just remember to include that URL on your marketing material and on your website.

New potential customers

You could simply run ads on Facebook and Twitter to your target audience announcing your app. Just spend a few bucks a day and let the campaign roll for a month or two. Google gives you a couple of great ways to promote your app.

- First, run an AdWords campaign to show up at the top of a relevant mobile Google search (http://bit.ly/2R9WMwk).
- You can use Google's Display Network to drive installs of your app by advertising directly to users of another app (http://bit.ly/2R48lp8).
- Since a lot of people spend a lot of time on YouTube, you could run 'In-Stream' (sometimes known as 'Pre-Roll') ads on YouTube targeting videos that are about similar apps or topics source: http://bit.ly/2RbPY1C.

By being ultra-specific about your targeting (either by location, by topic or both) you can get the exact people you want to download your app without spending a fortune on ads.

Summary

Apps are cool and are all over the place. People download them like crazy and they are a great tool for talking directly with your customers.

But ...

Don't just jump into apps because they are the latest thing. You can do plenty to target mobile users without apps. Do your research before committing time and money to making a full app.

But if it makes sense for you to get one made, don't hesitate too much to get it done. Your competition might already be working on one, or worse have one done already. If they have, download them all and 'pick them apart'. What's good? What isn't? How can they be improved? Note all your ideas down and then implement them into your app.

When you develop it, be sure you take stock of all options and refuse to be overcharged. There are websites that will gladly take $10,000 and give you a 'web app' that cost them a few hundred to make.

Learn the lingo in this chapter for the different programming languages and you will already be a step beyond everyone else. Then if you don't just want to pay a company to do it, you can hire a coder (on any of the sites

I mentioned). If you do, spend time reading through previous project submissions to see if there are projects of a similar complexity to get a sense of how much yours could cost.

Once your labour of love is created, promote it to your target audience and, at the very least, to your existing clients and contacts. (This might also be a good time to break out those PPC skills you learned yesterday.)

Fact-check (answers at the back)

1. An app is:
a) Three-fifths of an apple ❑
b) An application run on a laptop ❑
c) An application run on a smartphone ❑
d) A technical term for a jump shot ❑

2. Why should you consider getting an app made?
a) 90 per cent of time on a mobile phone is spent within apps ❑
b) Retailers can generate conversions 3x higher from an app than a mobile website ❑
c) Both of the above ❑

3. Every company in every situation should get an app.
a) True ❑
b) False ❑

4. Which of these can an app do?
a) Take your blood pressure ❑
b) Count your steps ❑
c) Do a 3D analysis of your home and tell your square footage. ❑
d) Make your phone a flashlight ❑
e) Teach a foreign language ❑
f) Get someone to wash your dog ❑
g) All of the above and more ❑

5. What should your app do?
a) One thing well ❑
b) Five things OK ❑
c) 27 things terribly ❑

6. There are three kinds of apps:
a) Native, hybrid, web ❑
b) Webby, new, old ❑
c) Web 2.0, domain, social ❑
d) Darla, Marc, and Rheta ❑

7. The best way to get an app made is always to use an app developing company.
a) True ❑
b) False ❑

8. Some the alternative ways to get an app made are:
a) UpWork.com ❑
b) eLance.com ❑
c) EasyOutsource.com ❑
d) Guru.com ❑
e) Do it 100% yourself ❑
f) All of the above ❑

9. You should always get your app put into the app stores of Google/Apple.
a) True ❑
b) False ❑

10. The easiest part of developing an app is:
a) Promoting it ❑
b) Creating it ❑
c) Developing it ❑
d) Designing the look and feel ❑

FRIDAY

SMS direct marketing

We as consumers are being bombarded by marketing messages all day, every day. Depending on who you believe, we're exposed to anything between 500 and 5,000 marketing messages and of those 99 per cent have zero impact on us, which makes sense as we just don't have the time or energy to fully process that much information every day.

Our brain ends up 'subconsciously skipping' – it knows we're not really interested and for marketers and business owners, that's wasted time, effort and money trying to get a prospect's or customer's attention.

However for the savvy marketer (which you most certainly are, since you're reading this book) correctly using SMS as part of your online marketing mix could be the Holy Grail for breaking through all the 'noise'. More so than anything else we've discussed previously in this book: more than Facebook, Twitter, Google AdWords, even (in my opinion) email.

So today, I'm going to cover: what SMS is (in case you've never touched a mobile phone before), why it's imperative you add it as a marketing channel NOW, how to get people to willingly give you their mobile phone number, examples of ideas that work great, the technical bits and bobs you need in place, the legal elements you *must* have in place so you don't fall foul of the authorities and how to automate SMS marketing without spamming.

Shall we?

What is SMS marketing?

SMS (Short Messaging Service) is the proper name for 'text messaging' on a mobile phone and so SMS *marketing* is the practice of collecting your customers' mobile phone numbers to enable you to contact them to inform and educate them on your products, services and offers, just like you would with their email, fax or postal address back in the day.

So how does it work? There are a few ways business owners and marketers do it but the most popular is to set up a shortcode; a special five- or six-digit number to which a lead, prospect or customer can send a text message and receive an automated response back and the business owner can automatically capture the phone number to use in future communications.

You can buy a shortcode exclusively for your business (expensive) or you can buy keywords in an existing shortcode.

Shortcodes

Shortcodes are country-specific so, depending on where you're located and where your customers or clients are, may require some planning on your side of things as to whether you'll need just a single shortcode or a shortcode for each country.

Search for terms like:

- 'SMS shortcode providers [country]'
- 'shared SMS shortcode [country]'
- 'dedicated SMS shortcode [country]'

... to give you an idea of your options.

Once you have a customer's mobile phone number in a database you can repeatedly offer deals and special offers to them, continually driving them back to your business, increasing your sales and profits for very little additional expense.

Adding SMS marketing to the online marketing mix

Since you're reading this book you obviously understand that people are more mobile than ever before and it's getting more and more difficult to reach them via traditional means, let alone getting your message to break through the hundreds (if not thousands) of marketing messages the average person sees every day.

In 2016 62.9% of the world's population owned at least one mobile phone, forecasted to rise to 67% by 2019 and pass 5 billion people globally by 2020 (source: http://bit.ly/2ysZvFT). We're rapidly reaching a point where there will be hardly anyone on the planet who doesn't own a mobile phone and every single one of them can receive SMS messages, completely bypassing the marketing 'noise' around them.

In addition, SMS/text messaging has far better engagement than its older cousin, email.

- Email open rates (avg.): 22%
- SMS open rates (avg.): **98%**

- Email clickthrough rate (avg.): 7%
- SMS clickthrough rate (avg.): **14%**

- Email sales conversion rate (avg.): 2%
- SMS sales conversion rate (avg.): **8%**

- Email time delay to open (avg.): 384 minutes
- SMS time delay to open (avg.): **3 minutes**

TIP *I'm not advocating buying in lists of mobile numbers and spam-dialling them. That is most certainly not SMS marketing. You are going to build lists of people's phone numbers who have specifically requested to receive information from you.*

Later today we'll be discussing the legal requirements you need to observe so you don't run into the various government regulators who like nothing more than levying fines on unknowing business owners.

And finally, because there is a (albeit small) cost to send a text message, hardcore spammers tend to avoid it as it gets very expensive for them at scale. For instance, I can purchase an account at a bulk mailing service that allows me to send up to 2.5 million emails for $800 a month.

SMS message credits from bulk providers can cost anywhere between 1.5–5 cents per message so for 2.5 million mobile phone numbers it will cost anywhere between $37,500 and $125,000 to spam everyone in the database!

So you can see, it's a lot easier for spammers to generate profits from spending $800 than it is having to spend $125,000 – meaning on the whole, the signal-to-noise ratio for SMS marketing is very good since there isn't a ton of spam being received by users, increasing the chance of your message being seen and engaged with.

SMS list-building strategies

There are plenty of ways to ethically persuade users into giving you their mobile phone number. Here are a few:

Discount coupon

For example, if you were offering a 20 per cent discount coupon code you could say: 'Text GUIDE to 12345 to get 20% off your next order. Just show the unique discount code on your phone to the cashier and your 20% discount will be applied immediately!'

Or for service providers, 'Text AUDIT to 12345 to receive a free social media audit (worth $795) but only for the first 20 businesses so hurry!'

You can post signs promoting the offer around your shop, on your website, in your voicemail holding message; retailers, program your till to add it to every receipt.

Appointment reminders

This can either be a one-off reminder or a short series of texts, depending on how far out the customer is from the date. If they're a couple of weeks out you could have series of reminders as follows:

Immediate

'Hi [NAME], this is to confirm your appointment with [PERSON] is scheduled for [TIME] on [DATE]. Call [PHONE] if you need to cancel or reschedule.'

One week out

'Hi [NAME], just a reminder that in one week today, on [DATE] you have an appointment with [PERSON] at [TIME]. Call [PHONE] if you need to cancel or reschedule.'

Day before

'Hi [NAME], just a reminder that tomorrow, [DATE] your appointment with [PERSON] is at [TIME]. Call [PHONE] if you need to cancel or reschedule.'

The day (OPTIONAL)

'Hi [NAME], just letting you know that your appointment today with [PERSON] at [TIME] is still on. Call us on [PHONE] if you need to change the day or cancel. (No more reminders!)'

TIP *This is a great way of 'training' prospects and customers/ clients to receive on-going messages from you too!*

If you run regular online training/webinar events and your service doesn't support SMS reminders as part of their service, like GotoMeeting or WebinarJam, you could do it yourself. 'Text TRAINING5 to 12345 and I'll send you reminders on the day of the training/webinar so you don't miss it!'

Morning reminder

'Hi, this is Nick. Don't forget the Social Media Success online training starts at 3pm EST this afternoon. See you then!'

Final reminder

'Hi [NAME] The Social Media Success online training starts in 15 mins. Grab a coffee and I'll see you in a bit! P.S. Listen out for the surprise ;-)'

Contests and competitions

Everyone loves the chance to win something so why not organize a 'Text to enter' competition? The prize can be anything but try to make it relevant to your business and have a decent perceived value – something that your audience would genuinely love to win. If you're a retailer, you could offer a prize of $xxx to spend at your store. It will only cost you wholesale for the prizes and you're turning over stock.

Competition tips

TIP 1: Offer all entrants who don't win a one-time percentage discount coupon to drive people back to you and offset your prize costs.

TIP 2: Partner with non-directly-competing businesses and run a super-contest where the winner gets $xxx in store credit from each store? The prize could easily run into $ thousands. Tell each store owner to give a percentage discount coupon away to all non-winners to drive people back to their stores.

TIP 3: For the more entrepreneurial contest organizer, since you now have a list of mobile phone numbers in your system, you could:

● Offer the businesses the ability to market further special offers for a monthly fee + SMS costs. This idea works particularly well with businesses servicing a specific geographic area.

● Leverage the success of the first content and find more businesses to participate in another super-contest (offering further marketing afterwards for a reasonable monthly fee). Rinse, repeat.

Monthly newsletter

Publish a very simple monthly newsletter on a webpage on your website and send a link to the page every week/fortnight/month via text message.

Put some useful and interesting info (tips, tricks, money saving offers etc.) on there so people will want to receive the text message.

Put any contest details and legal info on the newsletter page. That will get people to click through to it.

Billing problems

You wouldn't strictly use an SMS list for this purpose, but it could allow you to potentially recapture lost revenue should a customer's credit or debit card fail to be billed, especially for service providers. Again this could be a series of text messages like:

Immediate

'Hi [NAME]. For some reason, we couldn't process your last payment for [ITEM/SERVICE]. There may be an issue with your payment method. Could you double check and let us know either at support@domain.com or call Accounting on [NUMBER] Thanks!'

Second reminder

'We've tried to process your billing for [ITEM/SERVICE] and it has failed again. Could you check or change your payment method so we can try once more? Help at support@domain.com or [PHONE]'

Final reminder

'Sorry. Your payment method has failed a third time and we've had to cancel [SERVICE]/pause your order. Contact the office on [PHONE] if you need any help.'

Customer surveys

This kills two birds with one stone. It gives you an excuse to capture a customer's mobile phone number but can also give you valuable feedback to improve how your business operates.

Offer a discount or an entry into a prize draw to win something as the 'carrot' for doing the survey and it's all good.

You can either use a service to handle the entire survey through text messages, or just capture the phone number and send a message with a link to a web-based survey that is mobile-responsive (automatically formats to fit a mobile phone's smaller screen).

TIP

FRIDAY

Immediate
'Thanks for your custom today. Would you be willing to take a short survey to improve our service? We'll give you a 20% discount coupon for helping. Text SURVEY to 12345 to begin.'

Example message 1
'How satisfied were you with the service you received today? Reply with the appropriate number.'
   1 – Very satisfied
   2 – Somewhat satisfied
   3 – Neutral
   4 – Dissatisfied
   5 – Very dissatisfied

Here's a great list of 30 SMS advertising examples: http://bit.ly/2ythjkt

And here are 42 SMS marketing templates to jumpstart your own messages: http://bit.ly/2yvnDHQ

Automated SMS marketing solutions

Trying to remain in constant contact with all your leads, prospects, customers and clients regardless of where they are in your sales 'pipeline' becomes an almost impossible task, especially when it's *you* servicing your customers and clients.

You don't want to have to think about hiring a full-time 'customer liaison' to do nothing but this but you don't see any other way.

One of the great things about mobile marketing in general and SMS marketing specifically is now technology has matured to the point where it's easy and cost effective to set up an automated SMS marketing system without having to sell your firstborn.

There are solutions now for every business size and budget: from the 'one man band' to a global multi-national corporation.

SMS delivery gateways

Regardless of what system you choose, you'll also need an account with an SMS Delivery Gateway. Normally when you send a text message from your phone, you connect with your mobile network and the message is sent directly via them to the recipient's phone. When you're using a third-party software or service, you're generally not able to directly connect to a mobile network since they're not being operated from a mobile phone with a mobile number. So, we need to link our software or service account to an SMS gateway which will route our text messages via their system and onto the mobile networks and eventually to the recipient's phone.

Depending on which country you're in and which countries you need to send SMS to will depend on the gateways you can choose from and the cost of each message – with International SMS being generally more expensive than domestic. Some gateways will allow you to buy SMS in bulk ahead of time to ensure you get the lowest cost possible.

I'd advise searching for terms like:

- 'bulk sms [your country]'
- 'bulk sms pricing [your country]'
- 'sms gateway [your country]'

Automated systems

There are various types of SMS automation systems out there. Some just do one job and many can handle multiple types of automation tasks. I've listed a few below to give you an idea of costing and functionality but there are many, many more out there.

As ever, spend a little time doing your due diligence before signing up to any service or buying any software. Speak to the companies to make sure there are no compatibility issues with the service or software working in your country.

If you need any help with this, feel free to email me on: nick@traxxon.co.uk and I'll try to steer you in the right direction.

Autoresponder systems

These allow you to schedule sequences of text messages ahead of time, configure delays between each automated message, group users into lists and assign sequences to them and more.

I've used http://textdeliver.com before and can recommend them and I've heard http://txt180.com is a good service as well but again, do your research first.

SMS marketing legalities

Each country has its own rules and regulations regarding how text messages can be used in a commercial setting and so before you do any SMS marketing you should research your country's specific legal requirements. Using a little common sense should mean you keep on the right side of the law, but it's best to know exactly what you can and can't do.

If you're intending to send commercial text messages across borders into different countries, it's also worth an email or a quick phone call to your regulatory body to clarify which country's law takes precedence. Is it the country your business is registered in, the location of the SMS service/server sending the texts, the location of the recipient or something else?

As an example of legal compliance, in the USA there is the Telephone Consumer Protection Act and there is also the CTIA, a non-profit body representing the wireless communications industry. To remain TCPA and CTIA compliant includes:

- storing each subscriber's data for a minimum of four years and that includes their phone number, IP address and any opt-in capture page URL)
- including your business name upon signup
- including the phrase 'Msg & Data Rates May Apply' upon signup
- appending T&C/Privacy Policy upon signup
- appending 'Opt-out' to each message (in bold)
- providing an 'Opt-out' confirmation message
- sending only between 8am and 9pm (relating to subscribers timezone)
- maintaining a DNC (Do Not Call/Do Not Message) list.

All common sense but nonetheless quite a bit to make sure you've taken into account.

Summary

SMS marketing is pretty cool isn't it?

Of all the techniques I have mentioned so far in this book, this is the only truly 'mobile' exclusive technique. If only for that reason this is one you must try if you are serious about reaching the mobile generation.

It really is a great way to break through the 'noise', as it were, since people are always (at least now) checking their SMS messages nearly constantly.

Investigate setting up either a dedicated or accessing a shared 'shortcode' number so you can have 'calls-to-action' like 'Text report to 12345'.

The ways to get numbers into your database is varied and limited only to your imagination. My personal favourite is the sweepstakes method, where you get them to enter based on what they can win. Make sure what they want to win is relevant to you as a business. If you give away an iPad, everyone and their uncle will be knocking at your door.

SUNDAY

MONDAY

TUESDAY

WEDNESDAY

THURSDAY

FRIDAY

SATURDAY

There are also many uses for SMS. For instance, you can remind someone of a meeting they made with you, or follow up with someone whose credit card was declined. This has great uses for getting webinar traffic, or getting people to your app (if you decided to build one yesterday). Anything that your customer *has* to know. It can also be used to run surveys and other direct methods.

We also looked at a bunch of technical things in this chapter, such as SMS gateways. We touched on legalities regarding SMS marketing too, lest you fall foul of the law.

Fact-check (answers at the back)

1. SMS stands for:
a) Save My Soul ❑
b) Short Messaging System ❑
c) Send Money Soon ❑
d) Sound Mantis Sting ❑

2. SMS gets opened:
a) 98 per cent of the time ❑
b) 50 per cent of the time ❑
c) 60 per cent of the time ❑
d) Never ❑

3. You need a shortcode provided in your country to get started on SMS marketing.
a) True ❑
b) False ❑

4. The best way to get numbers is to get a massive list and bulk dial them.
a) True (I like prison) ❑
b) False ❑

5. The way to get phone numbers the right way is:
a) Surveys ❑
b) % off promotions ❑
c) Contests ❑
d) All of the above ❑

6. A good idea for keeping in touch with potential clients using this technology is:
a) When you have a meeting with them. ❑
b) Their credit card was declined ❑
c) When you have a new contest running. ❑
d) When you have great promotions going on at your store. ❑
e) All of the above ❑

7. Running a survey via SMS is quick and easy
a) True ❑
b) False ❑

8. Getting an account with an 'SMS delivery service' is optional.
a) True ❑
b) False ❑

9. SMS marketing is completely unregulated and no one will ever get on you if you just start spamming people.
a) True ❑
b) False ❑

10. Automated survey and responses to queries is totally available with the tools I provided.
a) True ❑
b) False ❑

SATURDAY

The future of mobile marketing

A combination of ever-more powerful smartphones, costing less and less every year, connected to the internet by ever-increasing data speeds is fuelling a fundamental change in how we humans gather information and data for personal and commercial use.

Countries and locations where traditionally it wasn't cost-effective to supply phones and internet services could be helped by projects like Facebook's high-altitude solar powered 'Aquila' drone or their mesh network project to deliver high speed internet access on the ground without the need to build expensive infrastructure.

But as you and I know, time, tide and technology don't stand still and today I'd like to go over some of the newer mobile marketing concepts and ideas that are being discussed and in a few cases are already here, albeit in a very basic form.

I've picked the topics I believe to be the most important for you to begin investigating and implementing within your business or company over the coming weeks and months.

If during your research you can't find examples from others in your industry look to see what businesses in other markets have done with technologies and topics that could be tweaked for your own. Start thinking and strategizing your approaches now so you're ahead of your competitors ...

Mobile SEO (search engine optimization)

What is it?

Well, since we've already dedicated a whole day to it you should already know that it's the way of optimizing pages on your website to show in the Top 10 (and ideally the Top 3) results for a specific search term done on a mobile phone using Google's search engine.

Why is it important?

As I mentioned before, mobile *is* the internet now and with that comes changes to the ways that Google displays the results and which types of results to prioritize.

Since 2016 there have been several major updates to Google to follow their major 'Mobilegeddon' update in 2015, all of which are designed to further refine Google's index for mobile devices.

TIP *For more on Google Updates check out* **Search Marketing In A Week.**

Possum V1.0: An update that altered how Google displays businesses sharing a single location, as in serviced offices. There was also a ranking boost to businesses who were physically located just outside their operating town or city to enable them to begin to be seen in Google's 3-Pack results for a given area.

This is important since a 46% of all Google searches are local (i.e. 'emergency plumber Hoboken New Jersey') and of those 60% are people searching for local businesses using mobile search (source: http://bit.ly/2Oh8BAw).

In May 2016 Google gave a boost to websites that are 'mobile-friendly' and launched AMP (more details below) to deliver content quicker to users on mobile devices.

NOTE: Facebook also deployed their version of 'AMP' called Instant Articles which I'll also cover below.

And in direct response to the rise of mobile internet usage and mobile search as a whole, Google has begun to roll out its mobile-first primary index. This means regardless of what device you're using to perform a search – phone, tablet, or desktop – it will pull the results from the index gathered by its mobile-focused content spiders and ranked by its mobile-focused algorithm, rather than its 'traditional' desktop-focused database.

Because of this fundamental change to arguably the most powerful website on the internet, as I've mentioned previously it's essential your website is at best mobile-first or at least mobile-friendly to ensure it's still shown in search results.

Google realizes non-desktop internet usage is only going to increase and are focusing all their efforts into the various ways it's going to be used and you should too (so re-read this book at least three times and email me at nick@traxxon.co.uk if you have any questions).

Voice search

What is it?
It pretty much is what it sounds like: it enables you to perform searches on Google, Bing etc. just using your voice and your chosen device (mobile phone, Google Home, Amazon Alexa etc.) using natural language queries.

Why is it important?
After reading everything else in this book it will probably come as no surprise to you that voice searching in Google (whether using Google Assistant, Siri, Bixby or some other 'Intelligent Assistant') has dramatically increased.

It's estimated that 50% of all searches will be performed via voice by 2020 (source: comScore) and the number of households that own a 'smart speaker' like Google Home, Alexa, etc. will rocket from 13% to 55% by 2022 (source: OC&C Strategy Consultants).

Searches using 'Intelligent Assistants' have jumped from 'statistically zero' at the start of 2015 to an estimated 1 billion voice searches a month (source: Alpine.AI).

The search engines are starting to see a dramatic increase in longer, more complex queries with a more natural language structure and this is only going to increase as services and tools become much smarter in interacting with us.

Search queries are going to be less 'keyword' dependent and instead be more contextual. Google have said openly that:

'The destiny of [Google's search engine] is to become that Star Trek computer, and that's what we are building.'

Right now, you can do somewhat complex keyword-less searches on Google like: 'Which team won the Superbowl when was Richard Nixon President of the United States?'

Or

'Hey Google/Siri/Alexa/Cortana ... what's showing at the cinema tonight?'

'*Here are some films showing near you. What are you in the mood for?*'

'[FILM TITLE]'

'OK. Here are the times and locations nearby. Tap one and we can organize purchasing the tickets!'

With a little more technological progress it won't be long before you'll be able to search and make purchases just using your voice.

AMP (Google) and Instant Articles (Facebook)

What are they?

AMP (Accelerated Mobile Pages) is an open source project designed by Google and Twitter partnering with some of the largest content publishers online to formulate a web standard for mobile-optimized webpages that are created *once* and load instantly everywhere.

Facebook's Instant Articles project is a similar initiative to show content as quickly as possible for mobile devices via

Facebook but still have a visually rich display with high quality images and company branding and logos.

Think of them both as a stripped down, super-fast version of a regular page without a lot of bloated 'bells and whistles' code that can slow down the time it takes to render on a mobile device.

Both AMP and IA pages can also be cached by Google and Facebook respectively to their servers located around the world to ensure that the nearest server to a user will retrieve and display the content in question as quickly as possible.

Why are they important?

In a nutshell: bounce rate and page load time.

In layman's terms, bounce rate is described as the percentage of visitors to a page on your site who leave the site without loading another webpage or interacting with the site (like clicking a link).

Bounce rate is a major factor of Google's 'dwell time' calculations, 'dwell time' being the actual amount of time a user spends on a webpage before leaving it.

Google loves speed, so if a mobile user visits a page on a website that hasn't finished loading after 30 seconds (for example) then hits the 'Back' button on their browser, Google makes a note of that to say that page isn't mobile friendly and gives the site a 'black mark' against them. Too many black marks and that URL will either be penalized or Google will happily promote other more mobile-friendly websites above them, effectively pushing non-compliant sites down the rankings.

And it's the same principle for relevance: if a user visits a result from a specific topic and it's either not relevant or doesn't provide enough information, they'll leave the page quickly and Google makes a note that URL may not be relevant. Too many black marks and ... you know the rest.

In going forward with mobile marketing, AMP and Instant Articles, it is incredibly important that you maximize your page loading and dwell times because if Google is paying attention to this you can bet your bottom dollar Facebook is – and these factors will have an impact on their 'EdgeRank' algorithm as to whether your content will be seen more in people's Newsfeeds or not.

If you use Google Analytics, it's easy to specify the actual amount of time it takes to register a user as 'bouncing' from your site to minimize any false positives. Find an explanation and tutorial here: http://bit.ly/2R6yCD4.

Live streaming

What is it?
Live streaming is the ability to broadcast a live audio and/or video feed directly from your phone, tablet or desktop that the rest of the world can listen to or watch.

Why is it important?
Whilst live streaming has been around for quite a while, it required a little bit of techie knowledge to get up and running and it was only for streaming from a games console or desktop computer.

However, in 2015 a small company called Life On Air Inc. released an app called Meerkat that allowed anyone to livestream directly from their mobile phone just by clicking a button.

Thanks to its exposure at the South By Southwest festival in March 2015 and its ease of use, the app's popularity exploded and a slew of competitors suddenly appeared including Blab and Periscope. Within a few months:

- Periscope was bought by Twitter for $100 million
- Twitter shut off Meerkat's access to their social graph killing the app
- Blab also died due to ever mounting costs of running livestreaming servers without large amounts of venture capital
- YouTube and Facebook launched their own livestreaming functionalities.

Right now, livestreaming is in its infancy as a marketing platform but is maturing rapidly enabling companies to build ongoing relationships with prospects, customer and clients by educating and informing them in an entertaining way.

The key here is 'building ongoing relationships' with consumers. After the outcry over the spreading of so-called 'fake news' across Facebook, Mark Zuckerberg (Facebook's founder) shared that Facebook are implementing one of the largest changes to the news feed to prioritize content from friends over content from brands and businesses.

In case you didn't read his post, here's the direct link to it: http://bit.ly/2Odk3Nk (Facebook account required).

This means you can't just use Facebook as a passive broadcasting network, throwing up videos that get mass distribution. You need to provide genuine value to your audience and engage in conversation with them to ensure your video is seen and spread to as many of your target audience as possible.

The advantage of live video over pre-recorded content is it almost always generates conversation without trying – it's just the nature of the beast. People like feeling 'significant' in the eyes of others and so asking questions being mentioned in a live broadcast is an easy way for them to get that – which is great for you as you get engaging and interesting content for your broadcast.

The other benefit to livestreaming is, it's comparatively simple to do. There's no need for huge amounts of technical infrastructure. Just your phone and hitting the 'Live' button on your app.

For maximum reach you can stream on Facebook, YouTube, Instagram and Twitter all at the same time, just by setting up four smartphones with one of the apps on each and starting streaming at the same time.

TIP *If you intend to multi-stream using your home or office Wi-Fi connection, make sure your internet connection has a fast-enough upload speed to handle that many simultaneous live streams. Here's a chart that gives you a guideline to the sort of upload speeds you'll need according the quality output you want. http://bit.ly/2OgtHi9.*

If you intend to livestream using a phone's dataplan, it's worth doing a test stream for a few minutes and then checking your data allowance to get an idea of how long your livestreams will be over what timespan to make sure you don't go over your data cap.

There are online services that will syndicate your single livestream feed to other platforms at the same time but I don't have any experience using them so I can't testify as to how reliable they are:

● http://restream.io (free to 30+ destinations) with paid monthly upgrades)
● http://switchboard.live (paid monthly with additional plan upgrades) are two such services.

Restream does not natively support syndicating a livestream to Facebook for free but you can do it with their reasonably-priced paid plans.

Switchboard Live integrates syndicating a livestream to Facebook as part of their standard $10/m paid service.

So that's *how* you livestream, but *what* do you livestream?

No need to get super complex – there are a ton of things you can livestream. Here are a few to jumpstart your ideas:

● A regular Q&A livestream. Either take questions live at the time or get them sent to you beforehand.
● A behind-the-scenes at a special event. People love to see what's going on in the lead-up to an event, so show them. Don't just limit it to one or two times, do a whole series of livestreams covering different aspects of the event production.
● Related to the point above, if you're doing an event with multiple speakers, why not livestream an interview with a different speaker every week in the lead-up to the event. This will help to build up anticipation for the event and the speaker will most likely promote the interview to their subscribers and customers.
● Could you create a free training course related to your product or service? If so, then instead of using an expensive webinar provider like GotoWebinar, livestream it for free over Facebook, YouTube, Twitter etc.

Normally people would have to register with their email at the webinar-provider's URL to attend a webinar (which will likely interface with your email list provider like Aweber or Mailchimp building your email list) and you can do the same with livestreaming. All you do is schedule your live event(s) on Facebook, YouTube or whoever you're going to use ahead of time and paste the special web addresses into a textfile for use shortly.

Now you need to create a simple registration page hooked into your mailing list provider so you have somewhere to send prospective attendees and can automatically send them an email containing the URL they need to visit when you'll be broadcasting.

If you're a fancy pants tech person, then you can either create a simple page in HTML with Dreamweaver and FTP it up to your website. If you're not a geek, don't worry – there are plenty of services that can build you any type of page based on an existing template with just a couple of mouse clicks. All you have to do is edit the text on the page.

- http://clickfunnels.com
- http://leadpages.com
- http://megaphoneapp.com
- http://sendlane.com (these guys are actually an email service provider but they have their own landing page templates as well)
- If you use Wordpress, you can get a fantastic set of predesigned templates called Thrive Architect

These are all great and will integrate directly with most of the popular email service providers (apart from Sendlane – they are themselves an email service provider).

Or alternatively, use an SMS shortcode and autoresponder service like TextDeliver and have people send a text message asking to be notified when you're streaming live!

Chatbots/conversational commerce

What is it?

Conversational commerce (CC) was a term coined by Chris Messina in 2015 when discussing the use of messaging apps like Facebook Messenger, WhatsApp, WeTalk and 'Intelligent Assistants' like Siri, Cortana, GoogleNow, Viv etc. to interact with businesses and companies to perform tasks like 'get customer support', 'make a purchase', 'get personalized recommendations', etc.

Why is it important?

There are a couple of factors:

- With people spending more time on their phones, the limitation of the phone's screen size can sometimes make it difficult to purchase goods and services, especially with a retailer or service provider whose website is not optimized for mobile.
- Add to that messenger apps are becoming the preferred method of communication with the top three messenger apps – WhatsApp, Facebook Messenger and WeChat having a total of 4 billion users worldwide (source: http://bit. ly/2OguShz) and processing as many as 75 billion messages in a DAY (source: WhatsApp – New Years Day 2017).
- It's becoming clear that consumers are using chat from the very beginning of the customer journey (finding and researching products) all the way through to purchasing goods and services – all without leaving the chat app.

We know this because in the Far East, chatbots and CC is not a new technology. China's WeChat messaging app has been able to do all this and more for quite some time. Their 889 million active users can buy movie tickets, hail a cab, order food, send money to family and friends and much more – all without leaving the app: http://bit.ly/2R5uFyB.

Now, Western social media companies have finally woken up to the potential of supercharging the functionality (and thereby their revenues) of their messenger apps.

Facebook

Since FB spun Messenger off into its own app and released API access to its development platform over 200,000 developers have created more than 300,000 chatbots (and growing) being used in 200 countries.

Facebook are now also allowing companies to run Sponsored Message ads in Messenger to users who have an open and existing 'conversation' with the company AND anyone with a FB Ad account can also run a Newsfeed ad that takes people directly to a company Messenger chat.

Google

Because Google has two different messaging apps that basically do the same thing and a Chat service (similar to Apple's iMessage and Blackberry's BBM services) they're trying to persuade ISPs to use, none of their apps are anywhere near as popular as Facebook Messenger or WhatsApp and end up being a slightly nicer way to send and receive SMS and MMS messages.

The only useful thing you can do with Google and messaging are to run click-to-message (CTM) ads on mobile search which when clicked will trigger the text application on the user's device, prefilling the phone number and message so all the users have to do is click Send.

At its simplest, this CTM ad can come through to a dedicated customer support number where one of your staff can reply to the sender manually to keep the conversation going.

If you want to automate this, there are a few online chatbot builder services that will send and receive message via SMS like:

- Agent.ai
- Motion.ai
- Init.ai
- Reply.ai

And if you wanted to use this function to just build an SMS phone number list to promote and advertise to in the future, grab yourself phone numbers from Twilio.com and hook them into the TextDeliver.com service I mentioned yesterday on the SMS direct marketing chapter.

So the user flow would go:

C-T-M Google Ad → Twilio Number → TextDeliver → SMS List

As I said before, there are thousands of other chatbots/CC apps out there not just on Facebook and working with Google, but also Skype, Twitter, Slack, KiK and even email.

If you want to explore and see what bots are out there, here are four directories that between them should keep you busy!

- https://botlist.co
- https://www.botpages.com
- https://bots.directory
- https://botfinder.io

There's a lot more cutting-edge and future tech to start researching including: wearables, augmented reality/virtual reality, deep linking, proximity and contextual targeting and push notifications. Some are here now (push notifications) others are nearly here – but start reading up on them now to get ahead of the curve.

Summary

Wow, are you as jazzed about the future of mobile technology as I am right now?

Ok, maybe I am a geek but I bet if you have got to this point in your journey you're also thinking of some cool ideas for you and your business. There are so many opportunities out there right now it is insane.

But first and foremost, you need to ensure your website is mobile-first or mobile-friendly otherwise you risk never showing up in a Google search.

Voice search is not only going to be the future of mobile search but of search in general as it's the logical conclusion of how easy it can be made for consumers to search and purchase goods and services.

This makes it more important than ever to not only get your SEO on point, but also build up your company's branding so that people aren't asking smart speakers questions like 'I want an action camera that can livestream in 4K' but instead are saying 'Alexa, buy me a GoPro Hero7 Black.'

And if you are serious about using social media to build awareness about your brand, dip your toe into Livestreaming when you get a chance (once you've gotten going on the other things you have learned first).

In conclusion, focus on the other days (Monday–Friday) but be sure to keep all of the above on your radar and be ready to pounce when the time is right, you entrepreneurial tiger you!

Fact-check (answers at the back)

1. The future is mobile:
a) True ☐
b) False (I haven't actually read this book and skipped to the bottom) ☐

2. The Google 'Possum' update:
a) Helps businesses rank outside the centre of the city ☐
b) Helps clean up dead animals on the highway ☐
c) Plays dead when startled. ☐

3. What percentage of local searches in Google are done on a mobile device?
a) 40% ☐
b) 20% ☐
c) 60% ☐
d) 50% ☐

4. AMP stands for:
a) Attention Manic Peons ☐
b) Added Machine Placements ☐
c) Another Main Portal ☐
d) Accelerated Mobile Pages ☐

5. Getting your pages 'amp'ed:
a) Makes them look better ☐
b) Helps them sound better ☐
c) Helps them load faster ☐
d) Helps click faster ☐

6. Livestreaming helps you speak to large crowds of people in real time.
a) True ☐
b) False ☐

7. Video is taking off because:
a) Facebook is going all in ☐
b) Twitter bought and is promoting Periscope ☐
c) Google is promoting Youtube in their search engine all over the place. ☐
d) All of the above ☐

8. Livestreaming is mostly a simple affair.
a) True ☐
b) False ☐

9. The most chat messages sent in a single day via the What'sApp chat app was:
a) 10 billion ☐
b) 83 billion ☐
c) 75 billion ☐
d) 102 billion ☐

10. Chatbots are the future because of the answer to #9:
a) True ☐
b) False ☐

7 × 7

1 Dos of mobile marketing

- Make sure you are aiming at the right avatar and not just masses of Likes/fans; the quality of your prospects is almost always more important than the amount.
- Do make fun, engaging 'informative entertainment' content that the visitors you are hoping to attract want to stay and consume even with their limited attention span.
- Do keep to the highest standards possible in your products and services. Nothing can derail you faster than a few bad reviews on your Google My Business page.
- Do aim to be as detailed as possible in your customer avatar and keep changing it as you get to know your market better.
- Be social and have active social accounts on the networks your target prospects are on (search engines and real people like this). Remember YouTube/livestreaming is video and a source of good links and mobile traffic so use them as much as possible.
- Do PPC right, make sure you have an action that you are aiming for: visiting your home page doesn't count, the goal should be tied to something monetary as much as possible as well.
- Do constantly be testing, changing, and growing. Don't ever just settle for the status quo, always be setting yourself up for that next 'wave'.

2 Don't's of mobile marketing

- Don't try to find 'secret' PPC or other 'hacks' – most fail because they are short term loopholes and can get your Facebook Ad account banned once they close the loophole.
- Don't write bad or boring content for your visitors if you ever want to make sales from your efforts.

- Don't do anything without some kind of plan and an end game in sight.
- Don't outsource your work without fully making sure they understand what you are trying to accomplish.
- Don't set up your PPC campaigns and forget about them – constantly be checking them, running optimization reports and making changes.
- Don't do anything just to be 'different' – aim to follow time tested processes in similar niches to your own first before just trying something because it is new.
- Don't set up social accounts and then desert them with no interaction. This turns off mobile customers more than bad service.

3 Best tools and resources

- Adwords Keyword Planner: https://adwords.google.com/o/KeywordTool/
- Periscope for livestreaming: http://periscope.com
- BuzzSumo (http://buzzsumo.com) and EpicBeat (https://epicenter.epictions.com/epicbeat/#!/explore) to find interesting content on your topic to share with customers or comment on. Use the filters to find the most popular content (most liked, shared, engagement etc).
- 30 great types of SMS campaigns to run: http://bit.ly/2ythjkt
- Website Analytics Software: http://google.com/analytics
- Outsourcing: http://upwork.com
- Check and post to all your most important social accounts from one place here: http://hootsuite.com

4 Things to do this week (if you haven't yet)

- Set up your customer avatar.
- Check your website is mobile-friendly (look at it on a smartphone) and if not find someone on Upwork.com to fix it.

- Test it out and see if it is easy to find what you need. Add one-tap phone calls and email into your site.
- Set up your 'Google My Business'.
- Set up mobile social accounts where your customers are.
- Build your Facebook page and interact to start to learn what offers to make.
- Outsource anything you can (you could even have them do all of the above).

5 Things to do each business day

- Try to write every day, at least a fun status update or tweet or snap, even just a little bit. You will be amazed how it adds up over time.
- Write an email every day that would be good for your customer avatar (whether you send it or not).
- Check your analytics and see how people are reacting to content as you produce it. Do they come and immediately leave? Or do they stay and visit other pages?
- Set specific goals for mobile users of your site in Google Analytics (depending on the main action that you want them to take that leads to money for you) and check if the goals are being reached. If not something is wrong with your mobile setup.
- Set up a Google alert (google.com/alerts) to monitor new instances of your business name being mentioned, enabling you to instantly respond to any queries or potential problems.
- Check your Facebook/Adwords PPC campaigns and see if there are any changes needed.
- Check your social media accounts for any activity and respond to any questions or comments.

6 Things to do monthly (or occasionally)

- Check your website rankings in Google Webmaster tools. No need to do it daily as it's best not to give much credence to short term gains or losses but rather look at the big picture.
- Do a full audit of your Facebook/AdWords campaign and make sure any keyword, group or interest is profitable. Pause the ones that aren't.
- Update your avatar with something that you noticed in a customer interaction you had.
- Do a full audit of where visitors are landing on your site and where they are going. They might be landing in unexpected places for unexpected reasons.
- Change your goal values in Google Analytics to more accurately reflect how much money each action earns you.
- Check how many people are coming to you via your YouTube videos or social platforms and see if you can identify what made them click. Do more of that.
- Find your most popular mobile pages using analytics and make more pages like them.

7 Future mobile marketing trends to look out for

- Look for Facebook and Google to clamp down more and more on spam; don't ever try and get something over on them.
- Expect the unexpected, be willing to try anything out that shows even just a little bit of promise.
- Mobile Google ads will take more and more prominence; it is best to get in on these after you have mastered Facebook.
- Keep one eye on Snapchat – there seems to be definite increase in its older user base. While most of Snapchat's users are 18–24-year-olds there is an increase in the 25–34 demographic. Expect it to grow in power as a mobile market.

- Reviews will take more power for getting mobile traffic from Google and other sources, possibly even Facebook, so do your best to get good and solid reviews.
- Google is getting better at measuring the quality of a visitor's experience on your website every year. You must ensure your site is easy to navigate, and gives visitors the information they need to make informed decisions to move them closer towards the action you want them to take.
- Expect your customers' psychology to always be changing as new tech becomes available so always be learning more about how tech shapes minds and ideas.

Answers

Sunday: 1b, 2c, 3d, 4c, 5e, 6d, 7b, 8a, 9d, 10c
Monday: 1d, 2a, 3b, 4c, 5a, 6b, 7b, 8d, 9e, 10d
Tuesday: 1c, 2d, 3d, 4b, 5d, 6b, 7c, 8c, 9b, 10a
Wednesday: 1c, 2f, 3c, 4c, 5b, 6d, 7e, 8c, 9a, 10a
Thursday: 1c, 2c, 3b, 4g, 5a, 6a, 7b, 8f, 9a, 10a
Friday: 1b, 2a, 3b, 4b, 5d, 6e, 7a, 8b, 9b, 10a
Saturday: 1a, 2a, 3c, 4d, 5c, 6a, 7d, 8a, 9c, 10a